MATH

essentials

for the Pre-GED Student

David Alan Herzog

THOMSON

ARCO

Australia • Canada • Mexico • Singapore • Spain • United Kingdom • United States

THOMSON
™
ARCO

An ARCO Book

ARCO is a registered trademark of Thomson Learning, Inc., and is used herein under license by Peterson's.

About The Thomson Corporation and Peterson's

The Thomson Corporation, with 2002 revenues of $7.8 billion, is a global leader in providing integrated information solutions to business and professional customers. The Corporation's common shares are listed on the Toronto and New York stock exchanges (TSX: TOC; NYSE: TOC). Its learning businesses and brands serve the needs of individuals, learning institutions, corporations, and government agencies with products and services for both traditional and distributed learning. Peterson's (www.petersons.com) is a leading provider of education information and advice, with books and online resources focusing on education search, test preparation, and financial aid. Its Web site offers searchable databases and interactive tools for contacting educational institutions, online practice tests and instruction, and planning tools for securing financial aid. Peterson's serves 110 million education consumers annually.

For more information, contact Peterson's, 2000 Lenox Drive, Lawrenceville, NJ 08648; 800-338-3282; or find us on the World Wide Web at: www.petersons.com/about

ISBN: 0-7689-1253-9

Printed in the United States of America

10 9 8 7 6 5 4 3 2 1   05 04 03

First Edition

Contents

Section IV   Introduction to Algebra

Section V   Probability, Statistics, and Graphs

Section VI   Geometry

Section VII   Reevaluating Your Skills

Section VIII   Appendix

Introduction

You've taken a big step toward success on your GED by using this book. We know that you have a full, busy life and need a test-prep book that offers a fast and easy way to help you improve your math skills. We've created *Math Essentials for the Pre-GED Student* with that need in mind.

Many GED test-takers worry about taking the math section of the test because they are not confident about their math skills. Often, people who are preparing to take the GED look for a book to help them, but most GED prep books assume that readers have a high level of math skills. We know that's not always the case. This book will help you remember, or maybe even learn for the first time, the math skills you'll need for the GED.

About this Book

This book is broken down into five sections. Each section is divided into chapters that cover specific math topics. Before you dive into the chapters, take the pretest. The pretest has questions that each chapter covers, and your results on this will guide you to the topics that you really need to study. Following the pretest answers, you'll find a list that shows where each specific math topic you encountered on the pretest is explained in the book. You can study the entire subject covered in each chapter or go directly to the topics that you need to study.

Each chapter contains detailed explanations of different math topics and gives you the exact steps you need to take to solve the problems. At the end of each chapter, you'll find sets of practice exercises to help you review and practice what you learned in the chapter. The book ends with a posttest, so you can see whether you have learned the skills that you set out to learn.

Here's a brief description of what's in each chapter. If you see math words or phrases you don't understand, don't worry. You'll learn about all of these and more in this book.

Section I Working with Whole Numbers

- **Chapter 1** explains the process of addition in detail, including how to add great numbers.

- **Chapter 2** explains the steps of subtraction, including the process of "borrowing" or "renaming."

- **Chapters 3 and 4** cover multiplication. First is a review of multiplication facts and then a lesson in multiplying greater numbers together.

- **Chapters 5 and 6** deal with division and include the specific steps of dividing by one and two-digit numbers.

Section II Working with Fractions and Decimals

- **Chapter 7** explains the different uses and meanings of common fractions and mixed numbers. You're given examples of each use.

- **Chapter 8** looks at adding and subtracting fractions, writing equivalent fractions, and finding least common denominators and greatest common factors.

- **Chapter 9** explains multiplication and division of fractions. Division of fractions is then explained as "reciprocal multiplication"—a fancy name for using multiplication to divide fractions.

- **Chapter 10** introduces decimals and explains place value, how to multiply and divide by tens simply by moving the decimal point, and how to rename common fractions.

- **Chapter 11** explains adding, subtracting, multiplying, and dividing with decimals.

Section III Introduction to Algebra

- **Chapter 12** introduces you to algebra. The meanings of constants and variables are explained, and you'll learn how to solve basic equations.

- **Chapter 13** teaches you about the importance of "balance" in math and how to balance equations.

- **Chapter 14** covers ratios and proportions, teaches you to solve proportions by cross-multiplying, and covers basics of percents.

- **Chapter 15** teaches you how to solve problems that involve percent, how to find the percent of a number, and how to find percent discounts, simple interest, and sales tax.

Section IV Probability, Statistics, and Graphing

- **Chapter 16** examines the concept of probability or chance. You'll learn how to find simple probabilities with the help of common examples such as flipping a coin, rolling dice, and drawing a playing card at random.

- **Chapter 17** covers the basics of statistics by looking at different kinds of averages.

- **Chapter 18** explains a main use of statistics—putting together numerical information and presenting it in a graph or chart. It also explores pictographs, bar graphs, line graphs, and pie charts.

Section V Geometry

- **Chapter 19** introduces you to geometry, including points, rays, lines, segments, and angles. You'll also learn about the different types of triangles and quadrilaterals. A section on circles is included as well.

- **Chapter 20** shows you how to find perimeters and areas of triangles, rectangles, and circles. The chapter ends with an overview of coordinate geometry.

Let's Get Started

Once you feel comfortable with the types of questions you'll see on the test, you'll be more relaxed and confident when the time comes for you to take your GED Mathematics test. This book will help you fill in the gaps in your math knowledge and remind you of any math you have forgotten. Math can be challenging, but *Math Essentials for the Pre-GED Student* will help you meet that challenge. So, are you ready to start? Then turn to the Pretest and begin!

Evaluating Your Skills

Pretest

Take this Pretest to see how well you know basic math. Don't worry if you can't easily answer all the questions. The Pretest will help you understand which math skills you are already strong in and which skills you'll need to practice.

1. Write in words the value of the underlined digit: 2<u>6</u>,431,705

2. 3645 + 387 + 7230 + 6 =

Solve:

3.
$$\begin{array}{r} 647 \\ -\ 534 \\ \hline \end{array}$$

4.
$$\begin{array}{r} 2{,}358 \\ -\ \ 469 \\ \hline \end{array}$$

5.
$$\begin{array}{r} 4{,}003 \\ -\ \ 785 \\ \hline \end{array}$$

6.
$$\begin{array}{r} 689 \\ \times\ \ 7 \\ \hline \end{array}$$

7.
$$\begin{array}{r} 84 \\ \times\ 46 \\ \hline \end{array}$$

8.
$$\begin{array}{r} 798 \\ \times\ 46 \\ \hline \end{array}$$

9. $8\overline{)2376}$

10. $28\overline{)6354}$

Solve the following. Express answers in simplest form (where appropriate).

11. $\dfrac{3}{5} + \dfrac{1}{5} =$

12. $\dfrac{2}{3} + \dfrac{1}{6} =$

13. $\dfrac{5}{8} - \dfrac{1}{4} =$

14. $\dfrac{2}{3} \times \dfrac{3}{5} =$

15. $\dfrac{5}{6} \div \dfrac{5}{18} =$

16. $3\dfrac{1}{4} + 4\dfrac{1}{3} =$

17. $5\dfrac{4}{5} - 2\dfrac{3}{8} =$

18. $5\frac{2}{3} \times 3\frac{3}{5} =$

19. $5\frac{2}{3} \div 2\frac{3}{4} =$

Express the following fractions as decimals.

20. $\frac{3}{100}$

21. $\frac{17}{1000}$

22. $\frac{5}{8}$

23. $4\frac{4}{5}$

Express the following as common fractions in simplest form or as mixed numbers.

24. 2.7

25. 0.008

Solve the following:

26. 8.3 + .008 + .67 =

27. 52.36 − 23.89 =

28. 0.07 x 34 =

29. 2.31 x 0.0006 =

30. $0.07\overline{)6.986}$

31. $2.4\overline{)3801}$

Solve for x or y:

32. $x + 7 = 23$

33. $y + (-6) = -20$

34. $\frac{y}{4} = \frac{7}{11}$

35. $x = 36\%$ of 25

Solve:

36. Francesco gets a 25% discount on an $80 VCR. How much does he pay?

37. Hailee deposits $500 at 7% interest. How much money will she have in her account after one year?

38. At a farm, pigs are to cows in the ratio 2:3. If there are 40 pigs, how many cows are there?

39. A spinning arrow is at the center of a circle that is $\frac{1}{2}$ colored blue, $\frac{1}{4}$ colored red, and $\frac{1}{4}$ colored green.

What is the probability of spinning two greens in a row?

40. Ian scored 84, 65, 76, 76, 92, 75, and 85 on his math tests.

  a. What was his median grade?

  b. What was the mode of his grades?

  c. What was his mean grade?

Statements 41 through 45 refer to the graph below.

Small Farms in Mercer County (1995–2000)
 = 200 farms

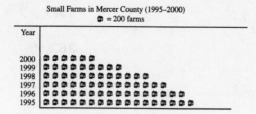

For each statement, choose "A" if the graph agrees with the statement, "B" if the graph contradicts the statement, or "C" if the graph neither agrees nor disagrees with the statement.

41. There were 600 fewer small farms in Mercer County in 1997 than in 2000.

42. In 2001, there will probably be 1000 small farms in Mercer County.

43. In 1999, there were 900 small farms in Mercer County.

44. Mercer County lost 1,100 small farms between 1995 and 2000.

45. The loss of small farms in Mercer County was probably due to grouping into large factory farms and changing of farmland to housing developments.

Answer the following questions:

46. What type of triangle is each marked to be?

a.

b.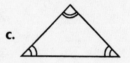

c.

47. Find the total number of degrees of angle measure in the figure below.

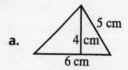

48. Find the area of each figure. Leave answers in terms of pi where appropriate:

a.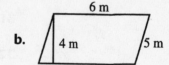

b.

6 m

4 m   5 m

c.

Answers

1. six million

2. 11,268

3. 113

4. 1,889

5. 3,218

6. 4,823

7. 3,864

8. 36,708

9. 297

10. 226 R26

11. $\dfrac{4}{5}$

12. $\dfrac{5}{6}$

13. $\dfrac{3}{8}$

14. $\dfrac{2}{5}$

15. 3

16. $7\dfrac{7}{12}$

17. $3\dfrac{17}{40}$

18. $20\dfrac{2}{5}$

19. $2\dfrac{2}{33}$

20. 0.03

21. 0.017

22. 0.625

23. 4.8

24. $2\dfrac{7}{10}$

25. $\dfrac{1}{125}$

26. 8.978

27. 28.47

28. 2.38

29. 0.001386

30. 99.8

31. 1583.75

32. $x = 16$

33. $y = -14$

34. $y = 2\dfrac{6}{11}$

35. $x = 9$

36. $60

37. $535

38. 60 cows

39. $\dfrac{1}{16}$

40.a. 76

b. 76

c. 79

41. B

42. C

43. B

44. B

45. C

46.a. isosceles

b. obtuse

c. equiangular

47. 360°

48.a. 12 cm²

b. 24 m²

c. 16π ft²

Pretest Item Reference Chart

This chart will help you focus your study on the items that you got wrong and even the items you got right but found difficult. The math topic covered by each question is listed below, along with page numbers to tell you where you can learn more about each type of question.

1. Reading place-value	Pages 52–54
2. Adding in columns	Pages 18–24
3. Subtracting without renaming	Pages 30–31
4. Subtracting with renaming	Pages 32–33
5. Subtracting with zeros on top	Pages 38–40
6. Multiplying by one digit	Pages 45–47
7. Multiplying by two digits	Pages 71–75
8. Multiplying greater numbers	Pages 75–77
9. One-digit divisors	Pages 91–97
10. Two-digit divisors	Pages 97–101
11-12. Adding fractions	Pages 111–120
13. Subtracting fractions	Pages 111–120
14. Multiplying fractions	Pages 133–135
15. Dividing fractions	Pages 136–139
16. Adding mixed numbers	Pages 121–124
17. Subtracting mixed numbers	Pages 125–128
18-19. Multiplying and dividing mixed numbers	Pages 139–141
20-23. Common fractions to decimals	Pages 150–154
24-25. Decimals to common fractions	Pages 150–154
26-27. Adding and subtracting decimals	Pages 157–159
28-29. Multiplying decimals	Pages 159–164
30-31. Dividing decimals	Pages 164–167
32-33. Solving algebraic equations	Pages 185–191
34. Solving proportions	Pages 195–197
35. Finding a percent of a number	Pages 205–206
36. Finding discounted price	Pages 206–209

Working with Whole Numbers

Addition | 1

Addition of Whole Numbers

When you add, you put together two or more amounts to get a greater amount. How do you know if a problem requires addition? You look for certain *key words* that let you know when a problem requires addition. Take a look at the following problem:

Frankie brought eight guests to the party, Rocio brought seven guests, and Kira brought four. Altogether, how many guests were brought to the party?

You can probably see that you are being asked to find the total number of guests brought to the party. The key word in this problem is the word **altogether**, which tells you that the problem will most likely need addition. Ask yourself whether the total will be more or less than the number of guests any one person brings. The total will be **more** since the number of guests that any one person brings is just a part of those who are brought **altogether**. That calls for a combining operation.

The next step is to recognize which combining operation is needed. Are the numbers to be combined the same? For instance, if each person brought four guests, you could use either multiplication (discussed in Chapter 3) or addition to find the total number of guests. In the problem above, the numbers are different. Since the numbers to be combined aren't all the same, you must add.

Add 8 + 7 + 4, and you'll see that 19 guests were brought to the party.

Now look at the problem below and see if you can find the key word that tells you what to do.

What is the sum of 9, 15, and 23?

The key word in the question above is **sum**. Sum is the name given to the answer of an addition problem. So, the word "sum" tells you that to find the answer to the problem, you must add. "In all" is another common phrase that indicates addition in word problems. Looking for the key words in word problems makes the problems much more simple.

Key Words for Addition			
total of	combined	added to	together
increased by	in all	more than	sum

Finding Sums Less Than Twenty

If you can add up to 18, you can add any two numbers in the decimal system. You'll learn more about decimals later on, but for now, know that the greatest addition problem in the decimal system is 9 + 9. You can see how this works in the following problem:

$$
\begin{array}{ccc}
3 & 3 & 7 \\
+\ 5 & 4 & 2 \\
\hline
\end{array}
$$

If you look at the numbers in total, it looks like you are being asked to add two numbers in the hundreds: three hundred and thirty-seven plus five hundred and forty-two. But you can make this addition problem simple by adding the columns one at a time, from right to left. Notice that none of the columns adds up to more than 9:

$$
\text{First}:
\begin{array}{ccc}
3 & 3 & 7 \\
+\ 5 & 4 & 2 \\
\hline
 & & 9
\end{array}
\qquad
\text{Next}:
\begin{array}{ccc}
3 & 3 & 7 \\
+\ 5 & 4 & 2 \\
\hline
 & 7 & 9
\end{array}
\qquad
\text{Finally}:
\begin{array}{ccc}
3 & 3 & 7 \\
+\ 5 & 4 & 2 \\
\hline
8 & 7 & 9
\end{array}
$$

You may be wondering what happens when the sum of the two numbers in a column is greater than nine. Well, when the sum of the two numbers is in between 10 and 18, you will have to "carry" or "carry over" some numbers. This topic is covered later in the chapter.

There are many clever shortcuts and different ways to do things in math (and this book is full of shortcuts), but there is no shortcut for learning the addition facts through 10. You need to know every sum of 10 or less without thinking about them. Complete the following Quick Quiz and time yourself. It shouldn't take you more than one minute to complete.

Quick Quiz A

Directions: Complete the following problems.

1. 2 + 3 = ___   **12.** 1 + 9 = ___

2. 4 + 3 = ___   **13.** 2 + 2 = ___

3. 5 + 2 = ___   **14.** 4 + 4 = ___

4. 4 + 6 = ___   **15.** 5 + 3 = ___

5. 3 + 5 = ___   **16.** 4 + 2 = ___

6. 6 + 4 = ___   **17.** 3 + 3 = ___

7. 8 + 2 = ___   **18.** 2 + 8 = ___

8. 2 + 7 = ___   **19.** 3 + 6 = ___

9. 2 + 5 = ___   **20.** 3 + 2 = ___

10. 5 + 5 = ___   **21.** 2 + 4 = ___

11. 3 + 4 = ___   **22.** 3 + 7 = ___

If you really know your addition facts through 10, the quiz above should have taken less than 30 seconds. If you took more than a minute or if you got any of the answers wrong, stop and make a set of flashcards with the questions above on the front and the answers on the back. This is one of the few things in math that needs to be absolutely perfectly memorized.

Once you know all the addition facts that sum to 10 or less, it's easy to deal with facts in the teens. Apply the facts that you already know to figure out those that you do not. Look at the following equation:

$$8 + 9 = \underline{}$$

Even if you already know what the sum is, follow along with the logic that's involved in solving the problem:

1) We are familiar with all sums to 10, and this isn't one of them. So, it makes sense that this sum is greater than 10.

2) If the sum is greater than 10, then it must be 10 plus something.

3) Looking at 8 + 9, we know that we must add 2 to the 8 to make 10. The 2 that we add to the 8 must come from the 9. When we take the 2 away from the 9, we are left with 7.

4) That means we can rewrite 8 + 9 as 10 + 7.

$$
\begin{array}{r}
10 \\
+\ 7 \\
\hline
17
\end{array}
$$

10 + 7 is 17:

Therefore, 8 + 9 = 17.

The only tricky part was in step 3. One of the numbers must be changed to a 10 by adding whatever number it takes to increase it to 10. In the case of 8, 2 more was needed for it to become 10. Of course, the 2 to be added to the 8 has to come from somewhere, and the only place for it to come from is the other number:

$$8 + 9 = (8 + 2) + (9 - 2) = 10 + 7 = 17$$

When the 2 is taken from the 9 to add to the 8, then only 7 of the 9 remains. 10 + 7 then makes a total of 17. The form of addition we just did is known as **grouping to ten**.

Quick Quiz B

Directions: Complete the following additions; group to 10.

1. 7 + 6 = 10 + ___   **7.** 3 + 8 = 10 + ___

2. 6 + 9 = 10 + ___   **8.** 9 + 4 = 10 + ___

3. 5 + 8 = 10 + ___   **9.** 5 + 7 = 10 + ___

4. 8 + 4 = 10 + ___   **10.** 4 + 7 = 10 + ___

5. 9 + 6 = 10 + ___   **11.** 7 + 9 = 10 + ___

6. 7 + 4 = 10 + ___   **12.** 8 + 6 = 10 + ___

Greater Sums

So far in this chapter, you have learned addition of small numbers. But what happens when you add greater numbers? In order to explain addition of numbers like 456 + 342, you need to understand the concept of **expanded notation**. Expanded notation is a way of writing numbers that spells out the value of the digit. Look at the following examples:

- 98 written in expanded form is 90 + 8.

- 76 written in expanded form is 70 + 6.

- 235 written in expanded form is 200 + 30 + 5.

Each digit is multiplied by the value of the place that it is in, and then the result is written down. In the example above, 235 is $(2\times100)+(3\times10)+(5\times1)$.

Quick Quiz C

Directions: Write the following numbers in expanded form.

1. 26 _____   **4.** 579 _____

2. 63 _____   **5.** 1,941 _____

3. 284 _____   **6.** 3,872 _____

Now you can use expanded notation to help you solve an addition problem with two greater numbers. Be sure to keep the columns lined up correctly. It is very important in addition to keep problems neatly lined up so that you don't accidentally add the wrong columns together.

Suppose we want to add 456 + 342. First, expand the two numbers:

$$
\begin{array}{rcccccc}
4 & 5 & 6 & \rightarrow & 400 & + \; 50 & + \; 6 \\
+ \; 3 & 4 & 2 & \rightarrow & 300 & + \; 40 & + \; 2 \\
\hline
 & & & & 700 & + \; 90 & + \; 8
\end{array}
$$

Next, we add the ones together, then the tens together, and then the hundreds together to get three partial sums, as shown above.

To get the answer back into place-value form (instead of expanded notation), add up the numbers from the partial sums. Remember to keep the place-value columns lined up correctly, starting from the right with the ones column. When the problem is set up correctly, no digit gets added to anything but zeros. This makes the addition simpler:

Correct:
$$
\begin{array}{r}
7 \; 0 \; 0 \\
9 \; 0 \\
+ \quad\; 8 \\
\hline
7 \; 9 \; 8
\end{array}
$$

Incorrect:
$$
\begin{array}{r}
7 \; 0 \; 0 \\
9 \; 0 \\
+ \quad 8 \\
\hline
2, \; 4 \; 0 \; 0
\end{array}
$$

Quick Quiz D

Directions: Complete the following problems.

1.
$$
\begin{array}{r}
2\ 3\ 4 \rightarrow 200 + 30 + 4 \\
+\ 1\ 5\ 3 \rightarrow 100 + 50 + 3 \\
\hline
\_\_ + \_\_ + \_\_ =
\end{array}
$$

2.
$$
\begin{array}{r}
3\ 8\ 9 \rightarrow 300 + 80 + 9 \\
+\ 6\ 1\ 0 \rightarrow 600 + 10 + 0 \\
\hline
\_\_ + \_\_ + \_\_ =
\end{array}
$$

3.
$$
\begin{array}{r}
5\ 3\ 2 \rightarrow 500 + 30 + 2 \\
+\ 4\ 5\ 6 \rightarrow 400 + 50 + 6 \\
\hline
\_\_ + \_\_ + \_\_ =
\end{array}
$$

4.
$$
\begin{array}{r}
4\ 4\ 3 \rightarrow 400 + 40 + 3 \\
+\ 2\ 5\ 4 \rightarrow 200 + 50 + 4 \\
\hline
\_\_ + \_\_ + \_\_ =
\end{array}
$$

5.
$$
\begin{array}{r}
6\ 2\ 5 \rightarrow 600 + 20 + 5 \\
+\ 2\ 4\ 3 \rightarrow 200 + 40 + 3 \\
\hline
\_\_ + \_\_ + \_\_ =
\end{array}
$$

In the examples above, none of the columns you added had a sum greater than 9. Now, we'll move on to a more difficult problem that involves sums of greater than 9.

Find the sum of 375 and 258. Just like before, add each place-value column.

$$
\begin{array}{r}
3\ 7\ 5 \rightarrow 300 + 70 + 5 \\
+\ 2\ 5\ 8 \rightarrow 200 + 50 + 8 \\
\hline
500 + 120 + 13 =
\end{array}
$$

The 120 and the 13 make this problem harder. 120 is a mixture of hundreds and tens. You only want tens in that position. The same is true for the ones column. You only want ones in that position. Right now you have 13, a mixture of tens and ones.

You can use expanded notation again to finish solving the problem.

$$500 \quad + \quad 120 \quad + \quad 13$$

$$500 \quad + (100 + 20) + (10 + 3)$$

The parentheses above are used to indicate the numbers that were expanded.

$$120 = 100 + 20, \text{ while } 13 = 10 + 3.$$

Next, regroup those numbers so that the hundreds can be combined and the tens can be combined. Parentheses are used to show the numbers that will be added together:

$$500 + 100 + 20 + 10 + 3$$

$$(500 + 100) + (20 + 10) + 3$$

Adding them, you get:

600 + 30 + 3, which equals 633.

This may seem to be a long process for adding two numbers. It isn't a method that's ordinarily used to solve addition problems, but it shows you how numbers can be grouped to make them easier to work with. Knowing how to regroup numbers can help you rework difficult problems to make them simpler.

Quick Quiz E

Directions: Solve the following problems in expanded form.

```
        4  8  5  →  ___  +  ___  +  ___
1.    + 2  6  3  →  200  +  60  +  3
      _____
                   ___  +  ___  +  ___  =(600+100)  +       +      =
```

```
        5  7  5  →  ___  +  ___  +  ___
2.    + 3  4  8  →  ___  +  ___  +  ___
      _____
                   ___  +  ___  +  ___  =  ___  +  ___  +  ___  =
```

```
        3  5  9  →  ___  +  ___  +  ___
3.    + 2  7  6  →  ___  +  ___  +  ___
      _____
                   ___  +  ___  +  ___  =  ___  +  ___  +  ___  =
```

```
        2  8  9  →  ___  +  ___  +  ___
4.    + 2  6  8  →  ___  +  ___  +  ___
      _____
                   ___  +  ___  +  ___  =  ___  +  ___  +  ___  =
```

```
        7  7  8  →  ___  +  ___  +  ___
5.    + 5  9  6  →  ___  +  ___  +  ___
      _____
                   ___  +  ___  +  ___  =  ___  +  ___  +  ___  =
```

Column Addition

No matter how many numbers you may want to add, it is impossible to add more than two at a time. Try it. Add 3 + 8 + 5. If you added the numbers in the order that they are written, then you:

- First added 3 + 8 and got 11

- Then added 11 and 5 to get 16

You might have added them in a different order, but you still added two at a time. When you add a longer column of greater numbers, you are still adding two at a time. Look at the following example:

```
21     First:  21                                          21
13            +13     Next:  34                            13
12             34           +12     Finally:  46    Then:  12
+33                          46                           +33
                                          +33             ____
                                          ____             79
                                           79
```

| No matter how many numbers are in an addition problem, you don't ever have to add more than two at a time. |

Renaming

You have already seen renaming, also known as regrouping or "carrying." You might recognize "carrying" as looking something like this:

$$
\begin{array}{r}
\overset{1}{2}4 \\
+\ 16 \\
\hline
40
\end{array}
$$

Here, the numbers 4 and 6 in the right-hand (ones) column have a sum greater than 9; the sum is 10. What do you do? Well, we put the 0 in the ones place (which is where it is in the number 10) and "carried over" the 1 to the left-hand (tens) column. Then, we added to the numbers already in that column (2 and 1) together, and then added the 1 that we carried over to get 4 (2 + 1 = 3; 3 + 1 = 4).

This process of "carrying over" is also known as *renaming*.

In earlier problems using expanded notation, you were actually renaming in a different way. Now you are going to see how to rename in columns. Remember to keep the place-value columns lined up correctly.

Follow this example:
$$
\begin{array}{r}
4\ 6 \\
+\ 3\ 9 \\
\hline
\end{array}
$$

First, mark the places (T for *tens* and U for *units,* meaning *ones*):
$$
\begin{array}{c|c}
T & U \\
\hline
4 & 6 \\
+3 & 9 \\
\hline
\end{array}
$$

Then, add up the units:
$$
\begin{array}{c|c}
T & U \\
\hline
4 & 6 \\
+3 & 9 \\
\hline
 & 15 \\
\end{array}
$$

You may have noticed that 15 is too great a number to be in the units place. 15 is 1 ten and 5 units. The key is to **rename** the ten extra units as one ten and write it in the tens column:

$$
\begin{array}{c|c}
T & U \\
1 & \\
\hline
4 & 6 \\
3 & 9 \\
\hline
 & 5 \\
\end{array}
$$

Next, the tens can be added:

$$
\begin{array}{c|c}
T & U \\
1 & \\
\hline
4 & 6 \\
3 & 9 \\
\hline
8 & 5 \\
\end{array}
$$

Then:
$$\begin{array}{r} 4\;6 \\ +\,3\;9 \\ \hline 8\;5 \end{array}$$

Notice again, we're using the word **rename,** instead of **carry,** because *renaming* is really what you are doing. You could also say you are regrouping. One ten is another name for ten ones, and ten ones can be regrouped into one ten. Either way, they are worth the same amount—ten.

Now you can take it one step further:

H	T	U
3	7	8
+ 2	9	5

First add the units:

H	T	U
3	7	8
+ 2	9	5
		13

10 of the 13 units must be renamed as 1 ten:

H	T	U
	1	
3	7	8
+ 2	9	5
	17	3

Next, the tens are added together:

H	T	U
	1	
3	7	8
+ 2	9	5
	17	3

Now there are 10 extra tens. They must be renamed as 1 hundred:

H	T	U
1	1	
3	7	8
+ 2	9	5
	7	3

Any time there are 10 or more in a single column, 10 must be renamed into the next column to the left. Then it becomes one of whatever that next column is. For example:

- 10 ones become 1 ten

- 10 tens become 1 hundred

- 10 hundreds become 1 thousand

The addition is completed by adding up the digits in the hundreds column:

H	T	U
1	1	
3	7	8
+ 2	9	5
6	7	3

Quick Quiz F

Directions: Complete the following problems.

1.

H	T	U
3	8	7
4	9	5

4.

H	T	U
4	5	3
3	9	9

2.

H	T	U
5	6	5
2	7	8

5.

H	T	U
4	6	8
3	3	5

3.

H	T	U
5	7	8
2	6	8

6.

H	T	U
3	6	8
5	9	6

More About Renaming

There is one more type of addition problem that you haven't tried. In all of the earlier problems, you renamed less than 20 units and less than 20 tens. Whenever you regrouped, you put a 1 into the next column to the left, never a 2 or 3. Some problems require renaming multiple groups of 10. For example:

$$
\begin{array}{r}
8\;9 \\
4\;8 \\
5\;9 \\
+\;9\;7 \\
\end{array}
$$

First add the units:

T	U
8	9
4	8
5	9
9	7
	33

You get a sum of 33. Thirty-three is 3 tens and 3 units.

The earlier problems were about renaming ten of anything as one in the next column to the left (ten ones = one ten, etc.). The same applies to **multiples of ten** (10, 20, 30, 40, 50, etc.). Any number ending in a zero is a multiple of ten. In the decimal system, there may never be a multiple of ten written in any single place-value column. If a sum contains a ten in a single place, you know to rename it as 1 in the next column to the left. Following the same principle:

- 20 ones become 2 tens

- 30 ones are 3 tens

- 40 ones are 4 tens, and so on

So the 33 units in the example become 3 tens and 3 units. The 3 tens are regrouped into the tens column:

1)

H	T	U
	3	
	8	9
	4	8
	5	9
	9	7
	29	3

2)

H	T	U
2	3	
	8	9
	4	8
	5	9
	9	7
	9	3

3)

H	T	U
2	3	
	8	9
	4	8
	5	9
	9	7
2	9	3

In step 2, the 29 tens are renamed as 2 hundreds and 9 tens. Since there are no other hundreds to add to the 2 hundreds, you can just bring the 2 down to your answer.

Quick Quiz G

Directions: Complete the following problems.

```
      H  T  U
      4  7  8
1.    3  9  5
```

```
      H  T  U
      5  6  7
2.    3  7  6
```

```
      H  T  U
      4  6  6
3.    4  3  5
```

```
      H  T  U
      5  7
      6     8
4.    8  9
      7  6
```

```
      H  T  U
      4  8
      6     3
5.    9  5
      5  4
```

You may add place-value headings to the following if you wish.

```
      5  8  9
6.  + 4  7  3
```

```
      2  8  6
7.  + 9  4  7
```

```
      7  5  8
8.  + 8  7  4
```

```
      6  9
      3  7
9.    5  4
    + 4  8
```

```
       8  6
       9  4
10.    6  5
     + 5  7
```

```
       5  4
       3  6
       9  9
11.    8  2
     + 6  9
```

```
       6  9
       7  5
12.    5  8  3
     + 4  9  5
```

If you still feel uncomfortable with your ability to do addition, go back to the sections that you found hard. It's a good idea to keep practicing addition, even as you work on other parts of this book. Make up extra exercises for yourself, and check your work using a calculator or a computer.

Answers to Quick Quizzes

Answers to Quick Quiz A

1. 5		**12.** 10
2. 7		**13.** 4
3. 7		**14.** 8
4. 10		**15.** 8
5. 8		**16.** 6
6. 10		**17.** 6
7. 10		**18.** 10
8. 9		**19.** 9
9. 7		**20.** 5
10. 10		**21.** 6
11. 7		**22.** 10

Answers to Quick Quiz B

1. 3		**7.** 1
2. 5		**8.** 3
3. 3		**9.** 2
4. 2		**10.** 1
5. 5		**11.** 6
6. 1		**12.** 4

Answers to Quick Quiz C

1. 20 + 6	**4.** 500 + 70 + 9
2. 60 + 3	**5.** 1000 + 900 + 40 + 1
3. 200 + 80 + 4	**6.** 3000 + 800 + 70 + 2

Answers to Quick Quiz D

1. 300 + 80 + 7 = 387	**4.** 600 + 90 + 7 = 697
2. 900 + 90 + 9 = 999	**5.** 800 + 60 + 8 = 868
3. 900 + 80 + 8 = 988	

Answers to Quick Quiz E

1. 600 + 140 + 8 =
(600 + 100) + 40 + 8 = 748

2. 800 + 110 + 13 =
(800 + 100) + (10 + 10) + 3 = 923

3. 500 + 120 + 15 =
(500 + 100) + (20 + 10) + 5 = 635

4. 400 + 140 + 17 =
(400 + 100) + (40 + 10) + 7 = 557

5. 1,200 + 160 + 14 =
1000 + (200 + 100) + (60 + 10) + 4 =
1374

Answers to Quick Quiz F

1. 882

2. 843

3. 846

4. 852

5. 803

6. 964

Answers to Quick Quiz G

1. 873

2. 943

3. 901

4. 290

5. 260

6. 1,062

7. 1,233

8. 1,632

9. 208

10. 302

11. 340

12. 1,222

Subtraction | 2

A First Look at Subtraction

Subtraction is used to find the difference between two amounts. A key word in subtraction is **difference.** Here is an example:

Bill is 19 years old, and Susan is 14. Find the difference *in their ages.*

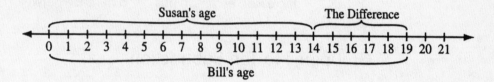

The first bracket on the top of the number line shows Susan's age, 14. The bracket on the bottom shows Bill's age, 19. The second bracket on the top marks the *difference* in their ages. By counting the spaces between their ages, you will find that the difference is 5. Another way to find the difference in their ages is to subtract 14 from 19: $19 - 14 = 5$. The minus sign (–) between two numbers means *subtract.*

Another key subtraction word is **remain.**

Here's an example:

Francesco got a check for $80. He paid a bill for $30. How much of his check remained?

This problem could be solved on the number line, just as the one about Bill's and Susan's ages was. But, you would need a very long number line to do that. Since you know *remained* means subtract, you can set up the problem as $80 - 30 = 50$. Francesco had $50 left.

Subtraction Facts

Assuming that you know your addition facts backward and forward, subtraction facts are simple since they are the reverse of addition facts. Take a look at the following "family of facts":

$4 + 5 = 9$	$5 + 4 = 9$
$9 - 5 = 4$	$9 - 4 = 5$

Figure out what number goes in the blank below:

$$3 + \underline{} = 8$$

You should get an answer of 5. How did you figure it out? For $3 + \underline{} = 8$, did you ask yourself "three plus what equals eight?" Or did you ask yourself, "Eight take away three equals what?" Both ways get you the same answer. Either way you did it, you were actually subtracting: $8 - 3 = 5$.

Key Words for Subtraction

less   decreased by   minus   difference between   fewer than

Groupings to Ten Subtraction

Since you should know all your addition facts through ten, there is no need to go into subtraction facts through ten. Subtraction is even easier than addition because you never need to subtract from a number greater than 18. Also, subtraction only involves two numbers at a time. There is no such thing as "column subtraction" the way there is column addition.

Subtraction always requires you to subtract a single number from another number, or to subtract a single number from a number in the teens, leaving you with a single number difference. Be sure to keep the digits in the units column lined up.

Quick Quiz A

Directions: Complete the following problems.

1. $\begin{array}{r} 7 \\ -\ 3 \\ \hline \end{array}$

2. $\begin{array}{r} 8 \\ -\ 5 \\ \hline \end{array}$

3. $\begin{array}{r} 9 \\ -\ 4 \\ \hline \end{array}$

4. $\begin{array}{r} 13 \\ -\ 6 \\ \hline \end{array}$

5. $\begin{array}{r} 14 \\ -\ 7 \\ \hline \end{array}$

6. $\begin{array}{r} 15 \\ -\ 8 \\ \hline \end{array}$

If you are not really sure of subtractions from the teens, there are two tricks that you can use:

1. **Try the problem as addition.** When you see $17 - 9$, think "9 plus what equals 17?" Use your addition facts to determine the answer.

2. **Figure out what you would need to take away in order to get to ten.** Then take the remaining amount away from ten.

Here is an example:

$$
\begin{array}{r} 17 \\ -\ \ 9 \\ \hline \end{array} \rightarrow \begin{array}{r} 17 \\ -\ \ 7 \\ \hline 10 \end{array}
$$

2 of the 9 remain to be subtracted: $\begin{array}{r} 10 \\ -\ \ 2 \\ \hline 8 \end{array}$

Therefore: $\begin{array}{r} 17 \\ -\ \ 9 \\ \hline 8 \end{array}$

Here is another example:

$$
\begin{array}{r} 18 \\ -\ \ 9 \\ \hline \end{array} \rightarrow \begin{array}{r} 18 \\ -\ \ 8 \\ \hline 10 \end{array}
$$ To get the 18 down to 10, take away 8.

1 of the 9 remains: $\begin{array}{r} 10 \\ -\ \ 1 \\ \hline 9 \end{array}$

Therefore $\begin{array}{r} 18 \\ -\ \ 9 \\ \hline 9 \end{array}$

Remember, if you are going to use this method, you should practice until it becomes very easy to you. When you take your GED exam, speed will count. Practice for speed and accuracy.

Quick Quiz B

Directions: Complete the following problems.

1.
14 →	14 →	10 →	14
− 6	− ☐	− 6	−
	10	8	☐

2.
13 →	13 →	10 →	13
− 7	− ☐	− 7	−
	10	6	☐

3.
15 →	15 →	10 →	15
− 6	− ☐	− 6	−

4.
16 →	16 →	10 →	16
− 9	− ☐	− 9	−

5.
12 →	12 →	10 →	12
− 5	− ☐	− 5	−

Subtraction Without Renaming

The easiest type of subtraction does not involve renaming. First you subtract in the units column. Then you move left to the tens columns and subtract there. If there are more digits, you keep moving left to the next column and subtracting until you have run out of digits. Look at three examples on the next page.

	Step 1	Step 2	Step 3

```
          4 5 6        4 5 6        4 5 6        4 5 6
1.      − 2 4 4      − 2 4 4      − 2 4 4      − 2 4 4
        ───────      ───────      ───────      ───────
                           2          1 2        2 1 2
```

```
          5 6 7        5 6 7        5 6 7        5 6 7
2.      − 3 0 4      − 3 0 4      − 3 0 4      − 3 0 4
        ───────      ───────      ───────      ───────
                           3          6 3        2 6 3
```

```
          6 7 8        6 7 8        6 7 8        6 7 8
3.      −   2 5      −   2 5      −   2 5      −   2 5
        ───────      ───────      ───────      ───────
                           3          5 3        6 5 3
```

Since there is no digit in the hundreds column in the bottom number in example 3, just move the 6 down into the answer.

You don't have to rename because the digit being "taken away" is always less than the digit it is being taken away from. In other words, the top digit in any place is always greater than the digit below it.

Quick Quiz C

Directions: Complete the following subtractions.

```
          5 9 7                          9 4 5
1.      − 3 8 4                 4.     − 3 4 2
        ───────                        ───────
```

```
          6 8 1                          5 6 3
2.      − 2 6 0                 5.     − 2 5 0
        ───────                        ───────
```

```
          8 8 5                          8 5 7
3.      − 5 2 5                 6.     − 8 4 5
        ───────                        ───────
```

Renaming to Subtract

The next challenge comes when one of the bottom digits is greater than the top digit. Look at the following subtraction:

$$
\begin{array}{r}
6\;5 \\
-\;2\;9 \\
\hline
\end{array}
$$

In this problem, there is no way to take 9 away from 5 without moving into negative numbers. To understand how to solve this type of subtraction problem, rewrite the numbers in expanded form:

$$
\begin{array}{rcl}
65 & = & 60 + 5 \\
-\;29 & = & -\;(20 + 9) \\
\hline
\end{array}
$$

The minus sign outside the parentheses is there to show that both the 20 and the 9 are being subtracted from the 65. (The 20 and the 9 are related to each other by the plus sign.) Notice that in the expanded form, the top numbers represent a total value of 65—exactly what we started with. You can group those numbers in any way you want as long as the total value of the top row is 65. Choose a new grouping that will help you subtract 29 from 65, and then rewrite the expanded numbers as follows:

$$
\begin{array}{rcl}
65 & = & 50 + 15 \\
-\;29 & = & -\;(20 + 9) \\
\hline
\end{array}
$$

The 60 + 5 has been renamed as 50 + 15. One full group of 10 was taken from the 60 and renamed as 10 units, then combined with the 5. The value of the top row is still 65. Now you can easily subtract.

- First, subtract the units column: $15 - 9 = 6$
- Then, subtract the tens column: $50 - 20 = 30$
- Last, combine those partial differences for the final answer: **30 + 6 = 36**

$$
\begin{array}{rcll}
50 & + & 15 & \\
-\;(20 & + & 9) & \\
\hline
30 & + & 6 & = 36
\end{array}
$$

This means that $65 - 29 = 36$.

Here's another example:

78	=		70	+	8	=		60	+	18	=		78
− 59	=	−	(50	+	9)	=	−	(50	+	9)	=	−	59
								10	+	9			19

Notice that the 9 of 59 cannot be subtracted from the 8 of 78. Instead:

- Expand the 78 and the 59

- Next, rename the 70 + 8 by subtracting a 10 from the 70 and adding it to the 8 units to make 18. The numbers still total 78. But, it has been renamed as 60 + 18.

- Then, you can subtract. We get a difference of 10 + 9, which, when added together, makes 19.

- So: **78 − 59 = 19**

Quick Quiz D

Directions: Complete the following problems.

1.
63	=	(60	+	3)	=		(50	+	__)
− 54	=	(50	+	4)	=	−	(50	+	4)
						__	+	__	= __

2.
74	=	(70	+	4)	=		(60	+	__)
− 48	=	(40	+	8)	=	−	(40	+	8)
						__	+	__	= __

3.
85	=	(80	+	5)	=		(70	+	__)
− 57	=	(50	+	7)	=	−	(50	+	7)
							+	__	= __

4.
41	=	(40	+	1)	=		(30	+	__)
− 29	=	(20	+	9)	=	−	(20	+	9)
							+	__	= __

5.
63	=	(60	+	3)	=		(__	+	__)
− 38	=	(30	+	8)	=	−	(__	+	__)
						__	+	__	= __

6.
72	=	(70	+	2)	=		(__	+	__)
− 45	=	(40	+	5)	=	−	(__	+	__)
						__	+	__	= __

Subtraction in Place-Value Form

Expanded form is a great way to learn how something works and to gain experience with using the concept of renaming. But it is too slow for regular use and for great numbers. Take a look at the following subtraction example to see how to use renaming in place-value form:

$$\begin{array}{r} 53 \\ -26 \\ \hline \end{array}$$

Remember, when we rename in addition, we often have to rename ten ones as one ten. When subtracting, the exchange goes the other way. We exchange 1 ten for 10 units. Just like addition, you have to keep the place-value columns lined up correctly.

	T	U			T	U			T	U
					6				6	
	7	5			7̷	15			7̷	15
1.	−3	9	2.		−3	9	3.		−3	9
									3	6

In step 1, tens and units headings are written over each place to remind you of the value of the digit beneath. In step 2, one of the 7 tens has been renamed as 10 units and added to the 5 units. That makes 15 units and leaves 6 tens in the tens place. Finally, in step 3, we subtract. First, subtract the units: $15 - 9 = 6$. Then subtract the tens: $6 - 3 = 3$. The answer is 36.

Here is another example:

	T	U
	7	
8 4	8̷	14
−4 7	−4	7

One ten from the 80 is renamed as 10 units and added to the 4 units that are already there. That makes a 14 in the units column. Subtract: $14 - 7 = 7$. Then, subtract 4 tens from 7 tens, and you get a difference of 3 in the tens column. That makes a total difference of 37.

Quick Quiz E

Directions: Complete the following subtractions. You can add column headings if you wish.

1.
$$
\begin{array}{r}
63 \\
-\ 27 \\
\hline
\end{array}
$$

4.
$$
\begin{array}{r}
52 \\
-\ 18 \\
\hline
\end{array}
$$

2.
$$
\begin{array}{r}
48 \\
-\ 39 \\
\hline
\end{array}
$$

5.
$$
\begin{array}{r}
85 \\
-\ 16 \\
\hline
\end{array}
$$

3.
$$
\begin{array}{r}
84 \\
-\ 26 \\
\hline
\end{array}
$$

6.
$$
\begin{array}{r}
91 \\
-\ 47 \\
\hline
\end{array}
$$

If you had trouble with this exercise, go back and review the examples and explanations. Then make up some more exercises, do them, and check your answers with a calculator.

Three Places in Place-Value Form

Three-digit numbers in subtraction are handled in place-value form the same way as two-digit numbers. The one difference is that another renaming may be needed. In that case, remember that 1 hundred can be renamed as 10 tens. Here's an example:

	H	T	U
1.	8	6	3
	−4	7	8

	H	T	U
		5	
2.	8	6	13
	−4	7	8
			5

	H	T	U
	7	15	
3.	8	6	13
	−4	7	8
	3	8	5

Step 1 names the subtraction that is to be performed. The place names (H, T, and U) are over each column for reference purposes. Note that the top digit is less than the bottom digit in both the tens and the units columns.

In step 2, 1 ten from the 6 tens has been renamed as 10 ones. That leaves a 5 in the top line of the "T" column and makes 13 in the top line of the "U" column. Subtract the numbers in the units column: $13 - 8 = 5$. These steps are the same as when we had two-digit numbers.

For step 3, regroup again since you can't take the 7 tens away from 5 tens. Rename one of the 8 hundreds as 10 tens. Add 10 tens to the 5 tens that are already there to make a total of 15 tens. Seven hundreds remain in the "H" place. Subtract the numbers in the tens column: $15 - 7 = 8$. Subtract the hundreds to finish the problem: $7 - 4 = 3$. The final answer is **385**.

Here is a second example:

H	T	U
5	4	2
−2	6	8

First, rename 1 ten as 10 ones; then subtract the units:

H	T	U
	3	
5	$\cancel{4}$	12
−2	6	8
		4

Now rename 1 hundred as 10 tens and subtract the tens and hundreds:

H	T	U
4	13	
$\cancel{5}$	$\cancel{4}$	12
−2	6	8
2	7	4

Quick Quiz F

Directions: Complete the following subtractions.

1.
H	T	U
3	5	6
−2	9	7

4.
H	T	U
7	2	4
−3	6	9

2.
H	T	U
4	3	2
−1	7	5

5.
H	T	U
8	1	2
−4	9	7

3.
H	T	U
5	6	3
−2	9	8

6.
H	T	U
6	4	6
−2	7	9

Quick Quiz G

Directions: Complete the following subtractions. You can add place names (H, T, U) if you want. Remember that not all places may need renaming. Rename only when the bottom digit in any column is greater than the top digit in the same column.

1.	347 − 188	**4.**	434 − 259
2.	456 − 357	**5.**	657 − 276
3.	348 − 289	**6.**	578 − 249

Zeroing in on the Top Number

Sometimes, the top number contains a zero. Follow along with these three examples to learn how to handle this kind of subtraction:

$$\begin{array}{r} 460 \\ -\ 197 \\ \hline \end{array}$$

Example 1.

There is no real difference between this problem and any other place-value subtraction.

First, rename 1 ten as 10 ones, and then subtract the units:

H	T	U
	5	
4	6̸	10
−1	9	7
		3

Rename 1 hundred as 10 tens and subtract the tens:

H	T	U
3	15	
4̸	6̸	10
−1	9	7
	6	3

Finally, subtract the hundreds column:

H	T	U
3	15	
4̸	6̸	10
−1	9	7
2	6	3

Example 2. $\begin{array}{r} 503 \\ -\ 247 \\ \hline \end{array}$

This problem is different. We need 10 units to add to the 3 units, but there *are no tens* in the tens place.

To get some tens in the tens place, you must first rename 1 hundred as 10 tens:

$$
\begin{array}{ccc}
^4 & & \\
5\!\!\!/ & 10 & 3 \\
-2 & 4 & 7 \\
\hline
\end{array}
$$

Now you have 10 tens from which to rename a ten and add to the 3 units. Subtract the units:

$$
\begin{array}{ccc}
^4 & ^9 & \\
5\!\!\!/ & 1\!\!0\!\!\!/ & 13 \\
-2 & 4 & 7 \\
\hline
 & & 6 \\
\end{array}
$$

No more renaming is needed, so subtract tens and hundreds:

$$
\begin{array}{ccc}
^4 & ^9 & \\
5\!\!\!/ & 1\!\!0\!\!\!/ & 13 \\
-2 & 4 & 7 \\
\hline
2 & 5 & 6 \\
\end{array}
$$

Example 3. $\begin{array}{r} 800 \\ -\ 356 \\ \hline \end{array}$

The answer to this subtraction is similar to the one used for example 2. Again, since there are no tens to rename as ones, we must first go to the hundreds and rename a hundred as 10 tens:

$$\begin{array}{ccc} \overset{7}{\cancel{8}} & 10 & 0 \\ -\ 3 & 5 & 6 \\ \hline \end{array}$$

Now there are 10 tens from which to rename 1 as 10 ones. Subtract units:

$$\begin{array}{ccc} \overset{7}{\cancel{8}} & \overset{9}{\cancel{10}} & 10 \\ -\ 3 & 5 & 6 \\ \hline & & 4 \end{array}$$

No more renaming is needed, so subtract tens and hundreds:

$$\begin{array}{ccc} \overset{7}{\cancel{8}} & \overset{9}{\cancel{10}} & 10 \\ -\ 3 & 5 & 6 \\ \hline 4 & 4 & 4 \end{array}$$

Quick Quiz H

Directions: Complete the following subtractions.

1. $\begin{array}{r} 708 \\ -\ 319 \\ \hline \end{array}$ 4. $\begin{array}{r} 780 \\ -\ 297 \\ \hline \end{array}$

2. $\begin{array}{r} 570 \\ -\ 453 \\ \hline \end{array}$ 5. $\begin{array}{r} 905 \\ -\ 462 \\ \hline \end{array}$

3. $\begin{array}{r} 800 \\ -\ 654 \\ \hline \end{array}$ 6. $\begin{array}{r} 3,002 \\ -\ 189 \\ \hline \end{array}$

It is good to practice as much as you can, so make up more subtraction problems with and without zeros on top. Solve them on paper, and check your work with a calculator.

Answers to Quick Quizzes

Answers to Quick Quiz A

1. 4

2. 3

3. 5

4. 7

5. 7

6. 7

Answers to Quick Quiz B

1.
$$
\begin{array}{c}
14 \\
-\ 6 \\
\hline
\end{array}
\rightarrow
\begin{array}{c}
14 \\
-\ \boxed{4} \\
\hline
10
\end{array}
\rightarrow
\begin{array}{c}
10 \\
-\ \boxed{2} \\
\hline
8
\end{array}
\rightarrow
\begin{array}{c}
14 \\
-\ 6 \\
\hline
\boxed{8}
\end{array}
$$

2.
$$
\begin{array}{c}
13 \\
-\ 7 \\
\hline
\end{array}
\rightarrow
\begin{array}{c}
13 \\
-\ \boxed{3} \\
\hline
10
\end{array}
\rightarrow
\begin{array}{c}
10 \\
-\ \boxed{4} \\
\hline
6
\end{array}
\rightarrow
\begin{array}{c}
13 \\
-\ 7 \\
\hline
\boxed{6}
\end{array}
$$

3.
$$
\begin{array}{c}
15 \\
-\ 6 \\
\hline
\end{array}
\rightarrow
\begin{array}{c}
15 \\
-\ \boxed{5} \\
\hline
10
\end{array}
\rightarrow
\begin{array}{c}
10 \\
-\ \boxed{1} \\
\hline
9
\end{array}
\rightarrow
\begin{array}{c}
15 \\
-\ 6 \\
\hline
9
\end{array}
$$

4.
$$
\begin{array}{c}
16 \\
-\ 9 \\
\hline
\end{array}
\rightarrow
\begin{array}{c}
16 \\
-\ \boxed{6} \\
\hline
10
\end{array}
\rightarrow
\begin{array}{c}
10 \\
-\ \boxed{3} \\
\hline
7
\end{array}
\rightarrow
\begin{array}{c}
16 \\
-\ 9 \\
\hline
7
\end{array}
$$

5.
$$
\begin{array}{c}
12 \\
-\ 5 \\
\hline
\end{array}
\rightarrow
\begin{array}{c}
12 \\
-\ \boxed{2} \\
\hline
10
\end{array}
\rightarrow
\begin{array}{c}
10 \\
-\ \boxed{3} \\
\hline
7
\end{array}
\rightarrow
\begin{array}{c}
12 \\
-\ 5 \\
\hline
7
\end{array}
$$

Answers to Quick Quiz C

1. 213

2. 421

3. 360

4. 603

5. 313

6. 12

Answers to Quick Quiz D

1.
$$\begin{array}{r}(50 + 13)\\ -\ (50 + \ \ 4)\\ \hline 0 + \ \ 9\ =\ 9\end{array}$$

4.
$$\begin{array}{r}(30 + 11)\\ -\ (20 + \ \ 9)\\ \hline 10 + \ \ 2\ =\ 12\end{array}$$

2.
$$\begin{array}{r}(60 + 14)\\ -\ (40 + \ \ 8)\\ \hline 20 + \ \ 6\ =\ 26\end{array}$$

5.
$$\begin{array}{r}(50 + 13)\\ -\ (30 + \ \ 8)\\ \hline 20 + \ \ 5\ =\ 25\end{array}$$

3.
$$\begin{array}{r}(70 + 15)\\ -\ (50 + \ \ 7)\\ \hline 20 + \ \ 8\ =\ 28\end{array}$$

6.
$$\begin{array}{r}(60 + 12)\\ -\ (40 + \ \ 5)\\ \hline 20 + \ \ 7\ =\ 27\end{array}$$

Answers to Quick Quiz E

1. 36

2. 9

3. 58

4. 34

5. 69

6. 44

Answers to Quick Quiz F

1.
H	T	U
2	14	
3̸	5̸	16
−2	9	7
	5	9

4.
H	T	U
6	11	
7̸	2̸	14
−3	6	9
3	5	5

2.
H	T	U
3	12	
4̸	3̸	12
−1	7	5
2	5	7

5.
H	T	U
7	10	
8̸	1̸	12
−4	9	7
3	1	5

3.
H	T	U
4	15	
5̸	6̸	13
−2	9	8
2	6	5

6.
H	T	U
5	13	
6̸	4̸	16
−2	7	9
3	6	7

Answers to Quick Quiz G

1. 159

2. 99

3. 59

4. 175

5. 381

6. 329

Answers to Quick Quiz H

1. 389

2. 117

3. 146

4. 483

5. 443

6. 2,813

Multiplication: The Basics | 3

Multiplying Whole Numbers

Multiplication is another combining operation. It is very similar to addition. In fact, multiplying is a shortcut for **adding the same number to itself over and over.**

$$7 + 7 + 7 + 7 + 7 + 7 = 6 \times 7 = 42$$

Six times seven is another way of writing $7 + 7 + 7 + 7 + 7 + 7$. The first number tells the number of times the second number is being added to itself. In this case, 7 is added to itself six times. The answer to a multiplication problem is called the product, which is 42 in this problem.

Any problem that can be solved by multiplication can also be solved by addition. Look at the example below:

Example 1. Kira, Hailee, Myles, Jakob, and Rocio each have 6 ice cream cones per week. How many ice cream cones do they have altogether in a week?

Multiplication solution: Addition solution:

$$
\begin{array}{r}
6 \\
\times\ 5 \\
\hline
30
\end{array}
\qquad\qquad
\begin{array}{r}
6 \\
6 \\
6 \\
6 \\
+\ 6 \\
\hline
30
\end{array}
$$

Not all combining operations can use multiplication. When different numbers are being combined, you must use addition. Multiplication can only be used to combine the same number over and over. See the example on the next page for a problem that can only be solved by addition.

Example 2. Sebastian has $150, Melissa has $256, and Frankie has $132. How many dollars do they have altogether?

Multiplication solution: Addition solution:

$$
\begin{array}{r}
\$\ 1\ 5\ 0 \\
2\ 5\ 6 \\
+\ 1\ 3\ 2 \\
\hline
\$\ 5\ 3\ 8
\end{array}
$$

None

Key Words for Multiplication

of   times   product of   multiply by   factor of

Multiplication Facts

The multiplications between 0×0 and 10×10 are known as the **basic multiplication facts.** You may have learned them as "times tables." All multiplying is built on these facts, so you have to really know them. To find out how well you know the multiplication facts, do Quick Quiz A and time yourself. It should not take you more than three minutes to finish all of them.

Quick Quiz A

Directions: Complete the following problems.

1. $1 \times 1 =$ ___ $2 \times 5 =$ ___ $3 \times 3 =$ ___ $4 \times 2 =$ ___ $5 \times 7 =$ ___

2. $5 \times 10 =$ ___ $1 \times 2 =$ ___ $2 \times 6 =$ ___ $3 \times 4 =$ ___ $4 \times 3 =$ ___

3. $4 \times 4 =$ ___ $3 \times 2 =$ ___ $1 \times 3 =$ ___ $2 \times 7 =$ ___ $5 \times 9 =$ ___

4. $3 \times 1 =$ ___ $2 \times 10 =$ ___ $4 \times 10 =$ ___ $1 \times 4 =$ ___ $2 \times 8 =$ ___

5. $2 \times 9 =$ ___ $5 \times 8 =$ ___ $3 \times 5 =$ ___ $4 \times 9 =$ ___ $1 \times 5 =$ ___

6. $1 \times 6 =$ ___ $3 \times 6 =$ ___ $4 \times 5 =$ ___ $5 \times 1 =$ ___ $5 \times 6 =$ ___

7. $3 \times 7 =$ ___ $1 \times 7 =$ ___ $4 \times 1 =$ ___ $5 \times 5 =$ ___ $2 \times 4 =$ ___

8. $5 \times 4 =$ ___ $3 \times 8 =$ ___ $1 \times 8 =$ ___ $2 \times 3 =$ ___ $4 \times 6 =$ ___

9. $4 \times 7 =$ ___ $2 \times 2 =$ ___ $3 \times 9 =$ ___ $1 \times 9 =$ ___ $5 \times 2 =$ ___

10. $2 \times 1 =$ ___ $3 \times 10 =$ ___ $4 \times 8 =$ ___ $5 \times 3 =$ ___ $1 \times 10 =$ ___

11. $9 \times 1 =$ ___ $8 \times 10 =$ ___ $10 \times 5 =$ ___ $7 \times 2 =$ ___ $6 \times 10 =$ ___

12. $8 \times 9 =$ ___ $9 \times 2 =$ ___ $10 \times 6 =$ ___ $6 \times 9 =$ ___ $7 \times 1 =$ ___

13. $7 \times 3 =$ ___ $10 \times 7 =$ ___ $6 \times 8 =$ ___ $9 \times 3 =$ ___ $8 \times 8 =$ ___

14. $9 \times 4 =$ ___ $6 \times 7 =$ ___ $7 \times 4 =$ ___ $8 \times 7 =$ ___ $10 \times 8 =$ ___

15. $6 \times 6 =$ ___ $10 \times 9 =$ ___ $9 \times 5 =$ ___ $7 \times 5 =$ ___ $8 \times 6 =$ ___

Many people believe that multiplication facts must be memorized. It helps to remember that the order of the numbers doesn't matter in multiplication. That means there are fewer facts to learn, since if you know 3×5, you also know 5×3. While it is a great idea to know the facts well, there are ways to learn them without strict memorization. You can use two-step multiplication anytime you happen to forget a multiplication fact. You can also learn to do more math in your head.

Two-Step Multiplication

It is important to remember that multiplying and adding are very similar. If you know certain multiplication facts, you can put them together to find ones you do not know. This chapter will review the easiest times tables. From those, you can build the others using two steps at a time.

The easiest multiplication facts are numbers multiplied by 1:

- **Multiplying by 1 is easy because one times any number is that number.**

In other words, $1 \times 1 = 1$, $1 \times 2 = 2$, $1 \times 3 = 3$, and so on.

The tens multiplication table is also easy:

- **To multiply any number by 10, add one zero to the end of the number.**

$10 \times 3 = 30$, $10 \times 12 = 120$, $10 \times 36 = 360$, and so on.

Multiplying by 2 is also known as doubling. Even if you aren't sure of the 2 times table, you probably know how to double numbers.

- **Just think of 2 times anything as adding the number to itself.**

$1 + 1$ (2×1), $2 + 2$ (2×2), $3 + 3$ (2×3), $4 + 4$ (2×4)

These are all examples of doubling and the 2 times table. Another method is counting by twos and keeping track of how many twos you've counted. For example, count 2, 4, 6, 8. You have counted twos four times, so 8 is 4×2 or 2×4.

The last table you *must* know is the 5 times table:

- **Counting by fives is a good way to learn and use the 5 times table.**

5, 10, 15, 20, 25, 30, and so on.

Note that any odd multiple of 5 ($1 \times$, $3 \times$, $5 \times$, and so forth) ends with a 5 (5, 15, 25, and so on). Any even multiple of 5 ($2 \times$, $4 \times$, $6 \times$, and so forth) ends with a 0 (10, 20, 30, and so on).

Do not read beyond this point if you do not know the 1 x, 2 x, 5 x, and 10 x tables! Go back and reread the information above, then practice these facts with flashcards.

Once you know the $1 \times$, $2 \times$, $5 \times$, and $10 \times$ tables, you can develop any other multiplication fact in two steps:

Desired fact: 3×8

Plan: $3 = 2 + 1$

Way to go:

$$
\begin{array}{rcccl}
 & 2 & \times & 8 & = & 16 \\
+ & (1 & \times & 8) & = & 8 \\
\hline
\text{Therefore:} & 3 & \times & 8 & = & 24
\end{array}
$$

Desired fact: 4×8

Plan: $4 = 2 + 2$

Way to go:

$$
\begin{array}{rcccl}
 & 2 & \times & 8 & = & 16 \\
+ & (2 & \times & 8) & = & 16 \\
\hline
\text{Therefore:} & 4 & \times & 8 & = & 32
\end{array}
$$

Desired fact: 6×8

Plan: $6 = 5 + 1$

Way to go:

$$
\begin{array}{rcccl}
 & 5 & \times & 8 & = & 40 \\
+ & (1 & \times & 8) & = & 8 \\
\hline
\text{Therefore:} & 6 & \times & 8 & = & 48
\end{array}
$$

Desired fact: 7×8

Plan: $7 = 5 + 2$

Way to go:

$$
\begin{array}{rcccl}
 & 5 & \times & 8 & = & 40 \\
+ & (2 & \times & 8) & = & 16 \\
\hline
\text{Therefore:} & 7 & \times & 8 & = & 56
\end{array}
$$

All multiplication facts between 1×1 and 7×10 can be found in either a single step or by a simple addition of two numbers. The 8 and 9 times tables could be found in the same way, but you would have to add the results of 3 multiplications together. For example:

$(5 \times) + (2 \times) + (1 \times)$ makes $8 \times$, and $(5 \times) + (2 \times) + (2 \times)$ makes $9 \times$.

You learned earlier that you could do any multiplying in two steps, not three steps. If you use subtraction (backward addition), you can find the 8 and 9 times tables in two steps. Look at the examples below:

Desired fact: 8×8

Plan: $8 = 10 - 2$

$$
\begin{array}{rrrrrr}
\text{Way to go:} & 10 & \times & 8 & = & 80 \\
& - \ (2 & \times & 8) & = & 16 \\
\hline
\text{Therefore:} & 8 & \times & 8 & = & 64 \\
\end{array}
$$

Desired fact: 9×8

Plan: $9 = 10 - 1$

$$
\begin{array}{rrrrr}
\text{Way to go:} & 10 & \times & 8 & = & 80 \\
& - \ (1 & \times & 8) & = & 8 \\
\hline
\text{Therefore:} & 9 & \times & 8 & = & 72 \\
\end{array}
$$

Two-step multiplication has two purposes. The first purpose is to help you really learn the basic multiplication facts. In order for you to succeed with harder multiplication and division, you have to memorize the multiplication facts. If you don't, multiplication and division problems will take you a long time to solve. To be successful on the GED exam, you have to be able to work quickly. Two-step multiplication lets you work with multiplying before you've learned all of your multiplication facts.

The second purpose of two-step multiplication is to make it easier for you to "solve problems in your head." More about solving problems in your head is covered later in this book.

Quick Quiz B

Directions: Complete the questions using only $1 \times$, $2 \times$, $5 \times$, and $10 \times$ tables or combinations of them:

1.

4×6:

$\square \times 6 = \square$

$+ (\square \times 6) = \square$

$4 \times 6 = \square$

4.

8×7:

$\square \times 7 = \square$

$- (\square \times 7) = \square$

$8 \times 7 = \square$

2.

7×7:

$\square \times 7 = \square$

$+ (\square \times 7) = \square$

$7 \times 7 = \square$

5.

9×7:

$\square \times 7 = \square$

$- (\square \times 7) = \square$

$9 \times 7 = \square$

3.

3×9:

$\square \times 9 = \square$

$+ (\square \times 9) = \square$

$3 \times 9 = \square$

6. $3 \times 7 =$

7. $4 \times 9 =$

8. $7 \times 6 =$

9. $6 \times 9 =$

10. $9 \times 9 =$

Use of Commas

Before we show you how to multiply tens, you need to learn about the use of commas and how to read greater numbers. You may have noticed that sometimes, when numbers are greater than hundreds, commas are used. The purpose of placing commas in great numbers is to make them easier to read. The traditional rule for use of commas is simple:

- If a numeral contains four digits or more, start at the right, and for each group of three digits that you count, place a comma.

  Here's an example:

  Start with: 42369178

  Group from right into threes: 42 369 178

  Place commas: 42,369,178

Recently, there have been some changes to the system. Many people now only use commas when the number has five or more digits, although the rule of counting by threes from the right still applies. They'd write 5000, but would still write 70,000. You may feel more comfortable using commas after each group of three digits; that is fine because both methods are correct.

Reading Great Numbers

Many people find great numbers confusing and hard to read. There is a pattern to the way that numbers are written in the decimal system. That pattern is formed by the constant repeating of the first three place names: hundreds, tens, and units (ones).

Look at the number 328. Read 328 aloud. It is read "three hundred twenty-eight." Don't put an "and" between the "three hundred" and the "twenty-eight." The "and" is saved for fractions and decimals. 657 is read "six hundred fifty-seven." Try 593. Did you read it as "five hundred ninety-three"? Now, notice how the places are arranged:

Hundreds (H)   Tens (T)   Units (U)

The places occupied by the 3, 2, and 8 in 328, and by the 5, 9, and 3 in 593 would look like this:

$$
\begin{array}{ccc}
H & T & U \\
3 & 2 & 8 \\
5 & 9 & 3
\end{array}
$$

Remember, there was going to be a pattern formed by repeating hundreds, tens, and units, or, simply, H's, T's, and U's. Now, look at the number 531,789. Let's see how it fits under the repeating place-headings:

$$
\begin{array}{cccccc}
H & T & U & H & T & U \\
5 & 3 & 1 & 7 & 8 & 9
\end{array}
$$

If you follow the pattern of reading each digit from left to right and saying the name of the column head after it, you would read this numeral "five hundred thirty-one, seven hundred eighty-nine." That is not correct, but it is very close. The H's, T's, and U's are grouped into *periods*. Each period has a name so that you can tell them apart. The period furthest to the right is called the ones period. We never bother to say its name. Every other period beside the ones, however, must be named. The next period to the left is the thousands. If we put those period names into place, the number will look like this:

Thousands			Ones		
H	T	U	H	T	U
5	3	1,	7	8	9

Now try reading it from left to right, but after each period when you see the comma—except the ones period—say the period's name. You should have read "five hundred thirty-one *thousand*, seven hundred eighty-nine." Read the numbers in the left-most period as if you were reading a three-digit number;

then say the name of the period. Read the next three digits as if they were a three-digit number, and since it's the ones period, don't say the period's name.

Quick Quiz C

Directions: Read the following numbers and write them down in the left column.

Thousands			Ones			Write the number's name:
H	T	U	H	T	U	
		8	6	4	1	1._____
2	4,		4	3	9	2._____
	8	5,	3	1	6	3._____
4	3	6,	2	5	3	4._____
8	0	3,	5	0	7	5._____

Still Greater Numbers

Now you are ready for the next two period names. The next period to the left of the thousands is the millions. Notice that each period name is a thousand times the previous period's name. A thousand ones make a thousand, a thousand thousands make a million. A thousand millions are a billion, so it is the next period.

Billions			Millions			Thousands			Ones		
H	T	U	H	T	U	H	T	U	H	T	U
	6	0,	0	0	0,	0	0	0,	0	0	0

Try reading that number. You might read it as sixty billions, no millions, no thousands, no ones. Since there is no significant digit (a digit other than zero) after the billions period, nothing needs to be said other than "sixty billion."

Quick Quiz D

Directions: Identify the following numbers.

Billions			Millions			Thousands			Ones			
H	T	U	H	T	U	H	T	U	H	T	U	
					5,	3	7	8,	0	0	0	A _____
				4	8,	0	0	0,	0	0	0	B _____
			5	6	3,	4	7	4,	0	0	0	C _____
				2,	0	9	8,	0	0	0,	0	0	0	D _____
		4	3,	1	4	2,	9	5	0,	0	0	0	E _____
3	7	6,	2	5	0,	0	3	8,	6	0	9	F _____

Quick Quiz E

Directions: Below are several great numbers written in decimal form. There is no chart of periods or places. Try to name these numbers without looking back at the chart. Only refer to the chart if you can't answer the questions without it.

1. 752,000

2. 9,662,000

3. 79,569,007

4. 678,000,059

5. 2,676,596,768

6. 762,996

7. 87,205,007

8. 967,802,005,060

Multiplying Tens

Multiples of ten often are called **decades**, and 10, 20, and 30 are examples of decades. To multiply any number by ten, just place a zero after it. For example:

$$10 \times 5 = 50 \text{ and } 10 \times 23 = 230.$$

You can also multiply any decade by a single digit number in your head.

Example 1. $6 \times 20 = ?$

You know that $20 = 2 \times 10$. So you can rewrite this multiplication to look like this: $6 \times (2 \times 10)$

When two or more numbers are being multiplied together, the way they are grouped for multiplication does not affect the result. You can rearrange the numbers like this: $(6 \times 2) \times 10$

The parentheses tell you which multiplication to do first. Since $6 \times 2 = 12$, we now have 12×10. By placing a zero after the 12, we complete the multiplication: $12 \times 10 = 120$

Therefore, $6 \times 20 = 120$.

There is a shortcut that could have been used to solve example 1. Look at the two numbers, 6 and 20. To multiply them:

- Multiply the tens digit, 2, by 6, and then put a zero at the end

- $6 \times 2 = 12$

- Put a zero after the 12 and you have 120

Example 2. $5 \times 70 = ?$

Multiply 5×7: $5 \times 7 = 35$
Then put a zero at the end: **$5 \times 70 = 350$**

As in addition, only two numbers at a time can actually be multiplied. Try multiplying $2 \times 3 \times 2$ in your head, and you will see that you actually do two separate multiplications. It makes no difference which two of the three numbers you group together to multiply first.

Quick Quiz F

Directions: Multiply the following numbers.

1. 4×50 **4.** 3×60

2. 5×60 **5.** 8×30

3. 7×40 **6.** 5×80

When numbers are written in place-value form, it is easiest to place the zero first, and then multiply the numbers in this form:

$$
\begin{array}{r} 50 \\ \times \quad 5 \\ \hline \end{array} \rightarrow
\begin{array}{r} 50 \\ \times \quad 5 \\ \hline 0 \end{array} \rightarrow
\begin{array}{r} 50 \\ \times \quad 5 \\ \hline 250 \end{array}
$$

Here's another example:

$$
\begin{array}{r} 70 \\ \times \quad 4 \\ \hline \end{array} \rightarrow
\begin{array}{r} 70 \\ \times \quad 4 \\ \hline 0 \end{array} \rightarrow
\begin{array}{r} 70 \\ \times \quad 4 \\ \hline 280 \end{array}
$$

Quick Quiz G

Directions: Multiply the following numbers.

1.
$$
\begin{array}{r} 40 \\ \times \quad 3 \\ \hline \end{array}
$$
4.
$$
\begin{array}{r} 50 \\ \times \quad 7 \\ \hline \end{array}
$$

2.
$$
\begin{array}{r} 60 \\ \times \quad 2 \\ \hline \end{array}
$$
5.
$$
\begin{array}{r} 70 \\ \times \quad 6 \\ \hline \end{array}
$$

3.
$$
\begin{array}{r} 20 \\ \times \quad 4 \\ \hline \end{array}
$$
6.
$$
\begin{array}{r} 80 \\ \times \quad 9 \\ \hline \end{array}
$$

Multiplying by hundreds works the same way, but you need to place two zeros at the end.

$$7 \times 300 = 2,100$$

$$7 \times 3 = 21$$

$$21 \times 100 = 2,100$$

Following the pattern, you can also figure out how to multiply thousands.

Quick Quiz H

Directions: Complete the following problems.

1.
$$
\begin{array}{r}
400 \\
\times \quad 2 \\
\hline
\end{array}
$$

6.
$$
\begin{array}{r}
800 \\
\times \quad 5 \\
\hline
\end{array}
$$

2.
$$
\begin{array}{r}
600 \\
\times \quad 3 \\
\hline
\end{array}
$$

7.
$$
\begin{array}{r}
900 \\
\times \quad 9 \\
\hline
\end{array}
$$

3.
$$
\begin{array}{r}
200 \\
\times \quad 4 \\
\hline
\end{array}
$$

8.
$$
\begin{array}{r}
8,000 \\
\times \quad 7 \\
\hline
\end{array}
$$

4.
$$
\begin{array}{r}
500 \\
\times \quad 8 \\
\hline
\end{array}
$$

9.
$$
\begin{array}{r}
6,000 \\
\times \quad 6 \\
\hline
\end{array}
$$

5.
$$
\begin{array}{r}
700 \\
\times \quad 7 \\
\hline
\end{array}
$$

10.
$$
\begin{array}{r}
7,000 \\
\times \quad 9 \\
\hline
\end{array}
$$

You will learn more about multiplication in the next chapter. Once you have learned the basic multiplication facts, you can move on to multiplying greater numbers.

Answers to Quick Quizzes

Answers to Quick Quiz A

1. 1,	10,	9,	8,	35
2. 50,	2,	12,	12,	12
3. 16,	6,	3,	14,	45
4. 3,	20,	40,	4,	16
5. 18,	40,	15,	36,	5
6. 6,	18,	20,	5,	30
7. 21,	7,	4,	25,	8
8. 20,	24,	8,	6,	24
9. 28,	4,	27,	9,	10
10. 2,	30,	32,	15,	10
11. 9,	80,	50,	14,	60
12. 72,	18,	60,	54,	7
13. 21,	70,	48,	27,	64
14. 36,	42,	28,	56,	80
15. 36,	90,	45,	35,	48

Answers to Quick Quiz B

1.
$$4 \times 6: \quad \boxed{2} \times 6 = \boxed{12}$$
$$+ (\boxed{2} \times 6) = \boxed{12}$$
$$4 \times 6 = \boxed{24}$$

2.
$$7 \times 7: \quad \boxed{5} \times 7 = \boxed{35}$$
$$+ (\boxed{2} \times 7) = \boxed{14}$$
$$7 \times 7 = \boxed{49}$$

3.
$$3 \times 9: \quad \boxed{2} \times 9 = \boxed{18}$$
$$+ (\boxed{1} \times 9) = \boxed{9}$$
$$3 \times 9 = \boxed{27}$$

4.
$$8 \times 7: \quad \boxed{10} \times 7 = \boxed{70}$$
$$- (\boxed{2} \times 7) = \boxed{14}$$
$$8 \times 7 = \boxed{56}$$

5.
$$9 \times 7: \quad \boxed{10} \times 7 = \boxed{70}$$
$$- (\boxed{1} \times 7) = \boxed{7}$$
$$9 \times 7 = \boxed{63}$$

6.
$$3 \times 7: \quad 2 \times 7 = 14$$
$$+ (1 \times 7) = 7$$
$$3 \times 7 = 21$$

7.
$$4 \times 9: \quad 2 \times 9 = 18$$
$$+ (2 \times 9) = 18$$
$$4 \times 9 = 36$$

8.
$$7 \times 6: \quad 5 \times 6 = 30$$
$$+ (2 \times 6) = 12$$
$$7 \times 6 = 42$$

9.
$$6 \times 9: \quad 5 \times 9 = 45$$
$$+ (1 \times 9) = 9$$
$$6 \times 9 = 54$$

10.
$$9 \times 9: \quad 10 \times 9 = 90$$
$$- (1 \times 9) = 9$$
$$9 \times 9 = 81$$

Answers to Quick Quiz C

1. Eight thousand, six hundred forty-one
2. Twenty-four thousand, four hundred thirty-nine
3. Eighty-five thousand, three hundred sixteen
4. Four hundred thirty-six thousand, two hundred fifty-three
5. Eight hundred three thousand, five hundred seven

Answers to Quick Quiz D

1. A   5 million, 378 thousand
2. B   48 million
3. C   563 million, 474 thousand
4. D   2 billion, 98 million
5. E   43 billion, 142 million, 950 thousand
6. F   376 billion, 250 million, 38 thousand, 6 hundred 9

Answers to Quick Quiz E

1. 752 thousand
2. 9 million, 662 thousand
3. 79 million, 569 thousand, 7
4. 678 million, 59
5. 2 billion, 676 million, 596 thousand, 768
6. 762 thousand, 996
7. 87 million, 205 thousand, 78
8. 967 billion, 802 million, 5 thousand, 60

Answers to Quick Quiz F

1.	200	**4.**	180
2.	300	**5.**	240
3.	280	**6.**	400

Answers to Quick Quiz G

1.	120	**4.**	350
2.	120	**5.**	420
3.	80	**6.**	720

Answers to Quick Quiz H

1.	800	**6.**	4,000
2.	1,800	**7.**	8,100
3.	800	**8.**	56,000
4.	4,000	**9.**	36,000
5.	4,900	**10.**	63,000

Advanced Multiplication 4

Beyond the Basic Facts

Once you know your basic multiplication facts, multiplying other numbers isn't hard. You're going to combine using your basic facts, multiplying by 10 and 100, and your addition skills to solve the problems in this chapter.

Multiplying Two Digits by One

There are many ways to multiply that will help you get the right answer (also known as the **product**). If you already know how to multiply two or more digits by two or more digits, use the method that you know. If you need help multiplying, try using the methods below. Here's an example:

$$\begin{array}{r} 48 \\ \times\ 7 \\ \end{array}$$ ←   This asks you to find the total of seven 48s.

This partial-products method uses the same idea of expanded notation that you used in addition and subtraction. You're going to multiply 7 by (40 + 8). Begin by multiplying 7×8.

$$\begin{array}{r} 48 \\ \times\ 7 \\ \hline 56 \\ \end{array}$$ is the result of multiplying 7×8. You still have to multiply 7×40.

Remember, multiplying a decade requires multiplying the tens digit and then placing a zero at the end. (See "Multiplying Tens" in the previous chapter.)

You multiply 7×40 and get 280: $\begin{array}{r} 48 \\ \times\ 7 \\ \hline 56 \\ 280 \\ \end{array}$

Now add the two partial products together:

$$
\begin{array}{r}
48 \\
\times\ 7 \\
\hline
\end{array}
$$

Partial product: 56
Partial product: 280
Final product: 336

Quick Quiz A

Directions: Complete the following problems.

1.
$$
\begin{array}{r}
52 \\
\times\quad 6 \\
\hline
1\ 2 \\
\_\ \_\ 0 \\
\hline
\_\ 1\ 2
\end{array}
$$

5.
$$
\begin{array}{r}
68 \\
\times\quad 9 \\
\hline
\_\ \_ \\
\_\ \_\ \_ \\
\hline
\_\ \_\ \_
\end{array}
$$

2.
$$
\begin{array}{r}
36 \\
\times\quad 4 \\
\hline
\_\ 4 \\
\_\ 2\ \_ \\
\hline
\_\ 4\ \_
\end{array}
$$

6.
$$
\begin{array}{r}
59 \\
\times\quad 7 \\
\hline
\_\ \_ \\
\_\ \_\ \_ \\
\hline
\_\ \_\ \_
\end{array}
$$

3.
$$
\begin{array}{r}
48 \\
\times\quad 5 \\
\hline
4\ \_ \\
\_\ \_\ \_ \\
\hline
2\ \_\ \_
\end{array}
$$

7.
$$
\begin{array}{r}
94 \\
\times\quad 9 \\
\hline
\_\ \_ \\
\_\ \_\ \_ \\
\hline
\_\ \_\ \_
\end{array}
$$

4.
$$
\begin{array}{r}
68 \\
\times\quad 3 \\
\hline
\_\ \_ \\
\_\ \_\ \_ \\
\hline
\_\ 0\ \_
\end{array}
$$

8.
$$
\begin{array}{r}
75 \\
\times\quad 8 \\
\hline
\_\ \_ \\
\_\ \_\ \_ \\
\hline
\_\ \_\ \_
\end{array}
$$

Multiplying Two Digits by Two Digits

Multiplying by a two-digit number uses two more steps than multiplying by a one-digit number does. You can use the same partial product method that you used when you multiplied two digits by one digit, but you'll also have to multiply by the tens digit in the bottom number.

Expanded notation will help you understand the example below. Follow these steps:

$$\begin{array}{r} 45 \\ \times\,26 \\ \hline \end{array}$$

- First, break the 26 into 20 + 6.
- Next, multiply the 6 units × (40 + 5).
- Then, multiply the 20 × (40 + 5).
- Add up the partial products for the final product.

Follow along with the example:

$$\begin{array}{r} 45 \\ \times\,26 \\ \hline \end{array}$$

1. First do 6 × 5:

$$\begin{array}{r} 45 \\ \times\,26 \\ \hline 30 \end{array}$$

2. Then 6 × 40:

$$\begin{array}{r} 45 \\ \times\,26 \\ \hline 30 \\ 240 \end{array}$$

3. Next comes 20 × 5:

$$\begin{array}{r} 45 \\ \times\,26 \\ \hline 30 \\ 240 \\ 100 \end{array}$$

4. Last, 20 × 40:

$$\begin{array}{r} 45 \\ \times\,26 \\ \hline 30 \\ 240 \\ 100 \\ 800 \end{array}$$

$$
\begin{array}{r}
45 \\
\times\,26 \\
\hline
30 \\
240 \\
100 \\
800 \\
\hline
1{,}170
\end{array}
$$

5. Finally, add:

Quick Quiz B

Directions: Complete the following multiplications.

1.
$$
\begin{array}{r}
5\,4 \\
\times\,3\,6 \\
\hline
2\,4 \\
3\,0\,0 \\
\_\,\_\,\_ \\
\_\,\_\,0\,0 \\
\hline
\_\,\_\,\_\,\_
\end{array}
$$
$= 6 \times 4$
$= 6 \times 50$
$= 30 \times 4$
$= 30 \times 50$

2.
$$
\begin{array}{r}
6\,7 \\
\times\,4\,8 \\
\hline
\_\,\_ \\
\_\,\_\,0 \\
\_\,\_\,\_ \\
\_\,\_\,0\,0 \\
\hline
\_\,\_\,\_\,\_
\end{array}
$$
$= 8 \times 7$
$= 8 \times 60$
$= 40 \times 7$
$= 40 \times 60$

3.
$$
\begin{array}{r}
7\,3 \\
\times\,5\,4 \\
\hline
\_\,\_ \\
\_\,\_\,0 \\
\_\,\_\,\_ \\
\_\,\_\,0\,0 \\
\hline
\_\,\_\,\_\,\_
\end{array}
$$
$= 4 \times 3$
$= 4 \times 70$
$= 50 \times 3$
$= 50 \times 70$

4.
$$
\begin{array}{r}
8\,5 \\
\times\,2\,4 \\
\hline
\_\,\_ \\
\_\,\_\,\_ \\
\_\,\_\,\_ \\
\_\,\_\,\_\,\_ \\
\hline
\_\,\_\,\_\,\_
\end{array}
$$
$= 4 \times 5$
$= 4 \times 80$
$= 20 \times 5$
$= 20 \times 80$

5.
$$
\begin{array}{r}
6\,9 \\
\times\,3\,6 \\
\hline
\_\,\_ \\
\_\,\_\,\_ \\
\_\,\_\,\_ \\
\_\,\_\,\_\,\_ \\
\hline
\_\,\_\,\_\,\_
\end{array}
$$
$= 6 \times 9$
$= 6 \times 60$
$= 30 \times 9$
$= 30 \times 60$

6.
$$
\begin{array}{r}
4\,3 \\
\times\,5\,8 \\
\hline
\_\,\_ \\
\_\,\_\,\_ \\
\_\,\_\,\_ \\
\_\,\_\,\_\,\_ \\
\hline
\_\,\_\,\_\,\_
\end{array}
$$
$= 8 \times 3$
$= 8 \times 40$
$= \_ \times 3$
$= \_ \times 40$

Two-Digit Multiplication Shortcuts

The problems in Quiz B were meant to help you better understand how two-digit multiplication works. Some people use the partial product method all the time, but there are some shortcuts that you can use, too. The most popular shortcut is multiplying by each digit in a single line. Here's an example:

$$
\begin{array}{r}
4\ 5 \\
\times\ 2\ 6 \\
\hline
\end{array}
$$

1. Multiply 6 × 5, but don't write the tens digit in the answer:

$$
\begin{array}{r}
3 \\
4\ 5 \\
\times\ 2\ 6 \\
\hline
0
\end{array}
$$

Note where the tens digit from 6 × 5 is placed.

2. Multiply 6 × 4, and add the regrouped 3 to the product:

$$
\begin{array}{r}
3 \\
4\ 5 \\
\times\ 2\ 6 \\
\hline
2\ 7\ 0
\end{array}
$$

6 × 4 = 24; then add 24 + 3 to get 27.

3. Put a placeholder zero in the units place before multiplying by 2 (tens):

$$
\begin{array}{r}
3 \\
4\ 5 \\
\times\ 2\ 6 \\
\hline
2\ 7\ 0 \\
0
\end{array}
$$

Since we next multiply by 2 tens, the answer has no units.

4. Multiply 2 × 5; notice where the digits are placed. Remember, you really multiplied 20 × 5.

$$
\begin{array}{r}
1\ \cancel{3} \\
4\ 5 \\
\times\ 2\ 6 \\
\hline
2\ 7\ 0 \\
0\ 0
\end{array}
$$

2 × 5 = 10

5. Multiply 2 × 4 and add the regrouped 1. You are really multiplying 20 × 40.

$$
\begin{array}{r}
1\ \cancel{3} \\
4\ 5 \\
\times\ 2\ 6 \\
\hline
2\ 7\ 0 \\
9\ 0\ 0
\end{array}
$$

2 × 4 = 8; 8 + 1 = 9

6. Finally, add the partial products:

$$
\begin{array}{r}
1\ \cancel{3} \\
4\ 5 \\
\times\ 2\ 6 \\
\hline
2\ 7\ 0 \\
+\ 9\ 0\ 0 \\
\hline
1\ 1\ 7\ 0
\end{array}
$$

Here is another example:

```
                 4              4
   5  6       5  6           5  6
              ↑
 × 4  7     × 4  7         × 4  7
              2             3  9  2
```

Before multiplying by 4 tens, put the placeholder "0" in the next row.

```
              2            2                    5  6
   5  6       5  6         5  6
                           ↑                  × 4  7
 × 4  7     × 4  7       × 4  7                3  9  2
   3  9  2    3  9  2      3  9  2
   0          4  0       2  2  4  0          + 2  2  4  0
                                              2  6  3  2
```

Each time you multiply (by either the ones or the tens digit), the top number is being treated as a single-digit number. In other words, 50 is treated as if it were 5. This is because the 10 times part of the 50 ($5 \times 10 = 50$) was taken care of when you placed the zero in the second line of the partial products.

Quick Quiz C

Directions: Complete the following problems.

```
           52                        87
         × 36                      × 63
         3 1 2                      _ 6 _
1.     _ _ _ 0               3.     _ 2 _ 0
       _ _ 7 2                      _ 4 _ _
```

```
           67                        98
         × 54                      × 75
         2 _ 8                      4 _ 0
2.     3 3 _ 0               4.     _ _ 6 _
       3 6 _ 8                      7 _ _ _
```

The following Quick Quiz will help you practice the skills just learned. Try to solve them the same way as the previous problems.

Quick Quiz D

Directions: Complete the following problems.

1. 84
    × 17

6. 25
    × 67

2. 78
    × 23

7. 84
    × 39

3. 69
    × 45

8. 76
    × 25

4. 97
    × 68

9. 89
    × 36

5. 86
    × 27

10. 58
    × 70

Multiplying Greater Numbers

Multiplying by greater numbers uses the same process, but you have to go through the steps more often. You should become comfortable doing multiplication of three-digit numbers by two-digit numbers, since that applies to multiplying money. Here's an example of three-digit times two-digit multiplication:

Example 1:   147
                  × 62

1. $\overset{1}{1}47$ ← Renamed
    × 62
    _____
    294   ←   2 × 147

2.   147
        × 62
        _____
        294
          0
    Place the "0." ↑

3. $\overset{2\,4}{1}47$
    × 62
    _____
    294
    8820   ← 6 × 147

4.   147
        × 62
        _____
        294
      +8820
        _____
        9114   ← Addition

You will probably solve greater multiplication problems with a calculator. It is easy to make mistakes when you multiply great numbers without a calculator.

In case you do have to solve a great multiplication problem with pencil and paper, here are some tips:

- Three-digit multiplication works almost exactly the same way as multiplying two digits.

- Since there are three digits in the multiplier (the bottom number), there will be three rows of partial products before the final addition.

- Since the second line in a two-digit multiplication problem begins with the placeholder zero in the units place, the third line begins with two placeholder zeroes.

- Since the third line is multiplication by hundreds, there will be zero ones and zero tens.

Example 2:
$$\begin{array}{r} 254 \\ \times\, 356 \end{array}$$

1.
$$\begin{array}{r} {}^{3\,2}\;254 \\ \times\, 356 \\ \hline 1{,}524 \end{array}$$
← Renamed

1,524 ← 6 × 254

2.
$$\begin{array}{r} 254 \\ \times\, 356 \\ \hline 1{,}524 \\ 0 \end{array}$$
Place the "0." ↑

3.
$$\begin{array}{r} {}^{2\,2}\;254 \\ \times\, 356 \\ \hline 1{,}524 \\ 12{,}700 \end{array}$$
12,700 ← 5 × 254

4.
$$\begin{array}{r} 254 \\ \times\, 356 \\ \hline 1{,}524 \\ 12{,}700 \\ 00 \end{array}$$
Place "00." ↑

5.
$$\begin{array}{r} {}^{1\,1}\;254 \\ \times\, 356 \\ \hline 1{,}524 \\ 12{,}700 \\ 76{,}200 \end{array}$$
76,200 ← 3 × 254

6.
$$\begin{array}{r} 254 \\ \times\, 356 \\ \hline 1{,}524 \\ 12{,}700 \\ +76{,}200 \\ \hline 90{,}424 \end{array}$$
← Addition

Quick Quiz E

Directions: Complete these larger multiplication problems.

1.
$$
\begin{array}{r}
436 \\
\times\ 65 \\
\hline
\end{array}
$$

4.
$$
\begin{array}{r}
247 \\
\times\ 53 \\
\hline
\end{array}
$$

2.
$$
\begin{array}{r}
240 \\
\times\ 12 \\
\hline
\end{array}
$$

5.
$$
\begin{array}{r}
351 \\
\times\ 45 \\
\hline
\end{array}
$$

3.
$$
\begin{array}{r}
532 \\
\times\ 34 \\
\hline
\end{array}
$$

6.
$$
\begin{array}{r}
167 \\
\times\ 185 \\
\hline
\end{array}
$$

Multiplication is an important, basic skill. If you can do the multiplication problems in this chapter, problems in later chapters will be much easier. Just like with addition and subtraction, you can get more practice doing multiplication by making up your own problems and checking your answers with a calculator.

Answers to Quick Quizzes

Answers to Quick Quiz A

1.
$$\begin{array}{r} 12 \\ 300 \\ \hline 312 \end{array}$$

2.
$$\begin{array}{r} 24 \\ 120 \\ \hline 144 \end{array}$$

3.
$$\begin{array}{r} 40 \\ 200 \\ \hline 240 \end{array}$$

4.
$$\begin{array}{r} 24 \\ 180 \\ \hline 204 \end{array}$$

5.
$$\begin{array}{r} 72 \\ 540 \\ \hline 612 \end{array}$$

6.
$$\begin{array}{r} 63 \\ 350 \\ \hline 413 \end{array}$$

7.
$$\begin{array}{r} 36 \\ 810 \\ \hline 846 \end{array}$$

8.
$$\begin{array}{r} 40 \\ 560 \\ \hline 600 \end{array}$$

Answers to Quick Quiz B

1.
$$\begin{array}{r} 24 \\ 300 \\ 120 \\ 1,500 \\ \hline 1,944 \end{array}$$

2.
$$\begin{array}{r} 56 \\ 480 \\ 280 \\ 2,400 \\ \hline 3,216 \end{array}$$

3.
$$\begin{array}{r} 12 \\ 280 \\ 150 \\ 3,500 \\ \hline 3,942 \end{array}$$

4.
$$\begin{array}{r} 20 \\ 320 \\ 100 \\ 1,600 \\ \hline 2,040 \end{array}$$

5.
$$\begin{array}{r} 54 \\ 360 \\ 270 \\ 1,800 \\ \hline 2,484 \end{array}$$

6.
$$\begin{array}{r} 24 \\ 320 \\ 150 \\ 2,000 \\ \hline 2,494 \end{array}$$

Answers to Quick Quiz C

1.
$$
\begin{array}{r}
52 \\
\times\,36 \\
\hline
312 \\
1{,}560 \\
\hline
1{,}872
\end{array}
$$

3.
$$
\begin{array}{r}
87 \\
\times\,63 \\
\hline
261 \\
5{,}220 \\
\hline
5{,}481
\end{array}
$$

2.
$$
\begin{array}{r}
67 \\
\times\,54 \\
\hline
268 \\
3{,}350 \\
\hline
3{,}618
\end{array}
$$

4.
$$
\begin{array}{r}
98 \\
\times\,75 \\
\hline
490 \\
6{,}860 \\
\hline
7{,}350
\end{array}
$$

Answers to Quick Quiz D

1. 1,428
2. 1,794
3. 3,105
4. 6,596
5. 2,322
6. 1,675
7. 3,276
8. 1,900
9. 3,204
10. 4,060

Answers to Quick Quiz E

1. 28,340
2. 2,880
3. 18,088
4. 13,091
5. 15,795
6. 30,895

Division: The Basics 5

Dividing Whole Numbers

Addition and multiplication are combining operations. They both combine lesser quantities to make greater quantities. Add $2 to $5, and you get $7, a quantity greater than either 2 or 5. If you have four $7 checks, you can find out the total amount of money by multiplying four by seven. Four times seven is 28, so you have a total of $28, an amount greater than either the four or the seven that you began with.

It makes sense that there should be two operations to undo the two combining operations addition and multiplication. Those "taking apart" operations are subtraction and division. With both subtraction and division of whole numbers, you start out with one quantity, and you end up with a lesser one. You learned about subtraction earlier in this book. In this chapter, you will learn about division.

Key Words for Division			
per	out of	ratio of	quotient

Division is related to two other operations: subtraction and multiplication. It is also known as the "undoing" of multiplication. For example, if 3 times 5 equals 15, then 15 divided by 5 equals 3. The sign '÷' is mathematical shorthand for "divided by."

Here are examples that show the relationship between multiplication and division. Study the example first, and then complete the Quick Quiz.

Example

$$3 \times 4 = 12 \qquad 4 \times 3 = 12$$
$$12 \div 4 = 3 \qquad 12 \div 3 = 4$$

Quick Quiz A

Directions: Complete the following problems.

1.
$5 \times 6 = 30$ $6 \times 5 = 30$
$30 \div 5 = \square$ $30 \div 6 = \square$

2.
$7 \times 9 = 63$ $9 \times 7 = 63$
$63 \div 9 = \square$ $63 \div 7 = \square$

3.
$8 \times 7 = 56$ $7 \times 8 = 56$
$56 \div 7 = \square$ $56 \div 8 = \square$

4.
$4 \times 6 = 24$ $6 \times 4 = 24$
$24 \div 6 = \square$ $24 \div 4 = \square$

5.
$3 \times 9 = \square$ $9 \times 3 = \square$
$27 \div 9 = \square$ $27 \div 3 = \square$

6.
$2 \times 8 = \square$ $8 \times 2 = \square$
$16 \div 8 = \square$ $16 \div 2 = \square$

Division has the same relationship to subtracting as multiplying does to adding:

- Multiplying is a way of doing repeated addition of the same number.

- Division is a way of doing repeated subtraction of the same number.

The division $42 \div 6$ may be thought of as asking, "How many times can 6 be subtracted from 42?"

$$42 \div 6 = ?$$

$$
\begin{array}{r|}
42 \\
\underline{-6} \\
36 \\
\underline{-6} \\
30 \\
\underline{-6} \\
24 \\
\underline{-6} \\
18 \\
\underline{-6} \\
12 \\
\underline{-6} \\
6 \\
\underline{-6} \\
0
\end{array}
$$

Count the number of 6s that were subtracted, and you'll see that there are seven of them. So the answer is: $42 \div 6 = 7$.

You can also think of division as breaking an amount of things into one or more equal groups. For example, what if a woman has $45, and she wants to give five equal gifts to her children? To find out how much she would give to each child, you would divide 45 by 5. Since $5 \times 9 = 45$, $45 \div 5 = 9$.

There are many different methods for doing division. If you already know one that works for you, keep using it. If you are not comfortable with division, this chapter will cover the basics so that you can move on to dividing greater numbers in later chapters.

Important Definitions

You will not find many technical terms in this book. But in some cases, knowing the technical terms and definitions will make your life easier. Three words about division are important to know. Look at the following diagram:

$$\text{divisor}\overline{)\text{dividend}}^{\text{quotient}}$$

1. The **divisor** is the number you *divide by*. It is on the outside of the division bracket.

2. The **dividend** is the number that *gets divided*. It is inside the division bracket.

3. The **quotient** is the *answer* to a division problem. It sits on top of the division bracket.

Here is an example of the diagram: $5\overline{)45}^{\,9}$

1. The divisor is 5.

2. The dividend is 45.

3. The quotient is 9.

Remainders

A remainder is what you get when one number does not divide into another an exact number of times. For example, when 7 is divided by 2, you find that three 2s fit into 7, and 1 will be left over. The number 1 is called the **remainder.** The word *remainder* is usually abbreviated by an "R," so you would write the answer as "3 R1" and say it as, "three, remainder 1."

Writing a remainder as a fraction was once taught as the "advanced" way to treat remainders. A fractional remainder can be written by placing the remainder above the divisor. Here's an example:

$$2\overline{)7}^{\,3R1} \qquad \text{or} \qquad 2\overline{)7}^{\,3\frac{1}{2}}$$

The so-called "advanced" way of writing remainders only as fractions is not used too often. Instead, the decision to write a remainder as a fraction or to leave it in the "R" form depends on the wording of the problem. Here are two problems with identical numbers. Read and solve each:

Problem 1. An electrician wishes to cut a 38-foot long wire into four equal parts. How long must each part be?

Problem 2. 38 students are to be seated equally at 4 tables. How many students will sit at each table? Will any students have to stand?

Problem 1 says that the wire must be cut into four equal lengths. Thirty-eight divided by 4 gives a result of 9 R2, but you can't have four 9-foot lengths of wire and a 2-foot length because then you have five pieces of wire. Instead, write the remainder as a fraction, so that each wire will be $9\frac{2}{4}$, or $9\frac{1}{2}$ feet long.

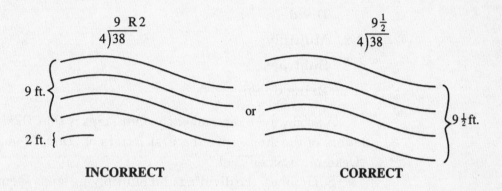

INCORRECT   CORRECT

The numbers in problem 2 are the same as those in problem 1, but the idea is different. You can't cut students in half to get an equal number at each table. 9 R2 is the needed solution. That means 9 students will sit at each table, and 2 will remain standing.

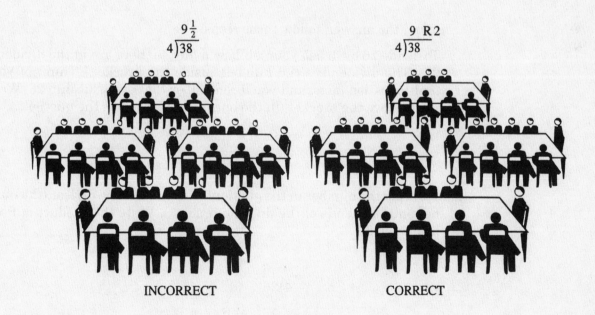

INCORRECT   CORRECT

One Step Beyond Basic Facts

The basic division facts are the multiplication facts backward. Remember that you can think of them using the missing numeral method. Instead of thinking "56 divided by 7 is what," think "7 times what is 56?"

Make flashcards if necessary and practice. Once you feel comfortable with basic divisions, you are ready for the basic rule for dividing greater numbers. Any form of division (not counting the basic facts) consists of repeating four steps. They are:

1. **Divide**

2. **Multiply**

3. **Subtract**

4. **Bring down**

A good way to remember the four steps is that D, M, S, and B—the first letters of the steps—are the first letters of "**D**ad, **M**om, **S**ister, **B**rother" or "**D**ead **M**ice **S**mell **B**ad."

Sometimes, the dividing and multiplying steps seem to only be one step. It may be hard to recognize that two separate steps have been done, but they always are. Here is a division example: $4\overline{)26}$

Read this as "26 divided by 4 equals what?"

You can also read it as, "How many 4s are there in 26?"

To find the answer, follow these steps:

1. To divide 26 by 4, ask yourself how many 4s there are in the dividend, 26. (The dividend is the number inside the bracket.) Think of your multiplication facts, and you'll remember that six 4s fit into 26. Write the 6 above the bracket (in the ones' place). The 6 is the quotient.

$$\overset{6}{4\overline{)26}}$$

2. Multiply the number in the quotient (the 6) times the divisor (the number on the outside of the division bracket). Write the product of 6×4 below the 26.

$$\begin{array}{r} 6 \\ 4\overline{)26} \\ \underline{24} \quad \leftarrow 6 \times 4 = 24 \end{array}$$

3. Subtract to find the remainder. The remainder could be zero.

$$
\begin{array}{r}
6 \\
4\overline{)26} \\
-24 \\
\hline
2
\end{array}
$$

4. Then write the remainder as shown:

$$
\begin{array}{r}
6 \quad \text{R2} \\
4\overline{)26} \\
\underline{24} \\
2
\end{array}
$$

The multiplying and dividing that took place in steps 1 and 2 are actually so tied together that it is hard at times to separate one from the other. The subtraction, on the other hand, is easy to see. The answer from the subtraction step should always be less than the divisor. If it is equal or greater, the quotient should be greater. Go back and redo the problem if that is the case. The fourth step of "bringing down" is not necessary in this problem.

Follow the steps in the model below:

$$
8\overline{)35} \longrightarrow \begin{array}{c} 8\overline{)35} \\ 8 \times \underline{} = 35? \end{array} \longrightarrow \begin{array}{c} 8\overline{)35} \\ 8 \times 4 = 32! \end{array} \longrightarrow \begin{array}{c} 4 \\ 8\overline{)35} \end{array} \longrightarrow \begin{array}{c} \times 4 \\ 8\overline{)35} \\ 32 \end{array} \longrightarrow \begin{array}{c} 4 \\ 8\overline{)35} \\ -32 \\ \hline 3 \end{array} \longrightarrow \begin{array}{c} 4\,\text{R3} \\ 8\overline{)35} \end{array}
$$

> Again, notice the steps: Divide, multiply, and subtract.

Quick Quiz B

Directions: Complete the following problems. Refer to the model if you need to. Express any remainders in "R" form.

1. $2\overline{)15}$ 7. $7\overline{)59}$

2. $3\overline{)17}$ 8. $8\overline{)67}$

3. $4\overline{)27}$ 9. $4\overline{)37}$

4. $5\overline{)31}$ 10. $5\overline{)39}$

5. $6\overline{)57}$ 11. $8\overline{)45}$

6. $9\overline{)81}$ 12. $6\overline{)43}$

You may have guessed that not all division problems are going to work out as easily as the ones above. Harder division problems are covered in the next chapter. Be confident about your multiplication and division facts before moving to the next section in this book.

Answers to Quick Quizzes

Answers to Quick Quiz A

1. 6, 5

2. 7, 9

3. 8, 7

4. 4, 6

5. 27, 27, 3, 9

6. 16, 16, 2, 8

Answers to Quick Quiz B

1. 7R1

2. 5R2

3. 6R3

4. 6R1

5. 9R3

6. 9

7. 8R3

8. 8R3

9. 9R1

10. 7R4

11. 5R5

12. 7R1

Advanced Division | 6

"Bringing Down"

Many division problems are harder than the ones covered in the previous chapter. However, all division problems use the same four steps:

1. Divide
2. Multiply
3. Subtract
4. Bring down

In this chapter, problems that use the "bring down" step are explained.

Bringing Down One Digit

'Bringing down' is necessary when the divisor divides the dividend more than 9 times. You need a way to divide by the divisor in each place-value column. Bringing down after the subtraction step allows you do to this. Follow along with the example on the next page to see how this works.

Example

$4\overline{)92}$ You must divide 92 by 4.

↓

$4\overline{)92}^{\,2}$ First, when you calculate $9 \div 4$, you will see that it
divides 2 times (i.e., two 4s fit into 9).

↓

$\begin{array}{r} 2 \\ 4\overline{)92} \\ 8 \end{array}$ Next, you multiply 2×4 and get a product of 8.
That means that the two 4s you have so far divided
account for 80 of the 92, since the 9 is in the tens place.

↓

$\begin{array}{r} 2 \\ 4\overline{)92} \\ -8 \\ \hline 1 \end{array}$ Now subtract and see that there is 1 (ten) left. But now, you have
to do something about that 2 still up next to the 9 in the dividend.

↓

$\begin{array}{r} 2 \\ 4\overline{)92} \\ -8\downarrow \\ \hline 12 \end{array}$ Bring the 2 down next to the 1 ten from your subtraction.
You have now gone through all 4 steps of the division process,
but the problem is not done. So you start back at step 1 again.

↓

Repeat the process, first dividing 12 by 4. Since there are three 4s in 12, multiply 4×3 and get a product of 12. Subtract and there is no remainder, so 92 divided by 4 equals 23.

$$\begin{array}{r} 23 \\ 4\overline{)92} \\ -8 \\ \hline 12 \\ -12 \\ \hline 0 \end{array}$$

You'll know that you've finished a division problem when you have no more digits to bring down from the dividend. Always make subtraction your last step. You'll either get a remainder of zero or a number less than the divisor.

Note that when you first divided by 4 and said that there are two 4s in nine, that wasn't really true. It was not really 9 but 90 that we were dividing by 4. When you multiplied, you placed the 8 beneath the 9, in the tens column, so that 8 was really worth 8 tens, or 80.

Quick Quiz A

Directions: Complete the following problems.

1. $3\overline{)54}$ 4. $4\overline{)92}$

2. $6\overline{)96}$ 5. $2\overline{)38}$

3. $5\overline{)85}$ 6. $7\overline{)98}$

Grouping Digits in the Dividend

Until now, we've been working with two-digit dividends and one-digit divisors. There are two possibilities that come up when a third digit is added to the dividend. The next examples explore both of those possibilities.

Example 1

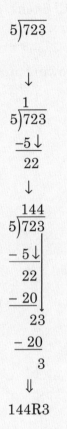

$5\overline{)723}$ Since 7 is greater than 5, everything proceeds as it did before...

$$5\overline{)723}$$
$$\begin{array}{r} 1 \\ 5\overline{)723} \\ -5\downarrow \\ \hline 22 \end{array}$$

$$\begin{array}{r} 144 \\ 5\overline{)723} \\ -\ 5\downarrow \\ \hline 22 \\ -\ 20 \\ \hline 23 \\ -\ 20 \\ \hline 3 \end{array}$$

...except that after the second subtraction, a second "bringing down" is needed.

$$144R3$$

Example 2

$9\overline{)345}$ Since 3 is less than 9,

$\downarrow$ the 3 is put together with the digit
to its right, and 34 is divided by 9.

$\begin{array}{r} 3 \\ 3\overline{)345} \\ -27\downarrow \\ \hline 7 \end{array}$ Notice that the 3 in the quotient is
written over the 4, *not over the 3,*
of the dividend.

$\downarrow$

$\begin{array}{r} 3 \\ 9\overline{)345} \\ -27\downarrow \\ \hline 75 \end{array}$

$\downarrow$

$\begin{array}{r} 38 \\ 9\overline{)345} \\ -27\downarrow \\ \hline 75 \\ -72 \\ \hline 3 \end{array}$ Everything else then goes on as it did before.

$\Downarrow$

38R3

Another possibility is that your quotient will contain a zero. If, after you subtract and bring down, the new number is smaller than your divisor, you'll get a zero in the quotient. The divisor goes into your new dividend zero times. Continue with the multiply, subtract, and bring down steps. You can see how this works in Example 3.

Example 3

$3\overline{)917}$ Since 9 is divisible by 3

$\downarrow$ (can be divided by 3),
         everything proceeds as it did.

$$3\overline{)917}^{\,3}$$

$-9\downarrow$
$\;\;0\;1$

$\downarrow$

$$3\overline{)917}^{\,30}$$

$-9\downarrow$
$\;\;0\;1$ But 3 divides 1 zero times . . .
-0
$\;\;\;1$

$\downarrow$

$$3\overline{)917}^{\,305}$$

$-9\downarrow$
$\;\;0\;1$
$-0\downarrow$ . . .so subtract and bring down
$\;\;17$ the 7. Now 3 divides 17 five times.
-15 Multiply and subtract, then you're done.
$\;\;\;2$

$\Downarrow$

305R2

When you practice, be sure to write your answers in remainder form or fraction form. Don't worry about using lots of paper and remember that you aren't finished with a problem until there are no numbers left to bring down from the dividend.

Quick Quiz B

Directions: Complete the following problems.

1. $4\overline{)275}$ 4. $6\overline{)734}$

2. $5\overline{)328}$ 5. $8\overline{)382}$

3. $4\overline{)827}$ 6. $5\overline{)875}$

Two-Digit Divisors

Up to this point, the division problems you've worked on only had single-digit divisors. Often, however, you will see two-digit divisors. The same four steps that you use for one-digit divisors you can use for two-digit divisors:

1. Divide
2. Multiply
3. Subtract
4. Bring down

These four steps are used as many times as needed, until all the digits of the dividend are brought down.

Take a look at the following example and you'll see that there is nothing really new in the process.

Example

$$25\overline{)462}$$

↓   As before, work the dividend one digit at a time, moving from left to right.

$$\begin{array}{r} 1 \\ 25\overline{)462} \\ -25 \end{array}$$

How many 25s are there in 4? None? Then put the 4 together with the 6.
How many 25s are there in 46? There's one, so we write one in the quotient above the 6. Then, we multiply, to find that 1 times 25 equals 25, which we write below the 46.

↓   (Since the one in the quotient is in the tens place, you're really multiplying 10 times 25 and getting 250, which you subtract from 462 to get 212.)

$$\begin{array}{r} 1 \\ 25\overline{)462} \\ -25 \\ \hline 21 \end{array}$$

Subtract, and you should have 21.

↓

$$\begin{array}{r} 1 \\ 25\overline{)462} \\ -25 \downarrow \\ \hline 212 \end{array}$$

Bring down the next digit from the dividend.

↓

$$\begin{array}{r} 18 \\ 25\overline{)462} \\ -25 \\ \hline 212 \\ 200 \\ \hline 12 \end{array}$$

Divide 212 by 25 (the hard part, since you must first estimate how many 25s are in 212) and find 8 of them.
Multiply 8×25 and get 200. Subtract.

⇓

18R12

Since there are no more digits to bring down, 12 is the remainder.

or

$$18\frac{12}{25}$$

The major difference between single-digit division and dividing by two-digit divisors is the difficulty of the division step. It isn't too hard to see that 4 divides 25 six times. The number of 25s there are in 212, however, is a much harder question. The trick is to estimate what the quotient will be: **about** how many 25s are there in 212?

To estimate a quotient, first look at the numbers with which the division is to be performed:

$$25 \qquad\qquad 212$$

Next, remove the right digit of each: 25 and 212 become 2 and 21.

How many 2s are there in 21? Since there are *about* ten 2s in 21, you can estimate that there will be ten 25s in 212. The answer that you get from estimating will get you close to the number you are looking for, but it's not usually the exact number. To find out how close you are, take your estimated ten and multiply it by 25, the actual divisor, to see how close you come to the actual dividend, 212:

$$10 \times 25 = 250$$

250 is greater than the 212 that you're looking for. That tells you that your estimated quotient, 10, is too great. Since ten 25s are too great, try nine 25s:

$$9 \times 25 = 225$$

That's still too great, so try eight 25s:

$$8 \times 25 = 200$$

Eight 25s is just the number you were looking for. It's almost 212 and isn't higher than 212.

In the examples below, you'll see two estimated quotients and then how those estimations are broken down:

Example 1

1. $23\overline{)187}$

    $\Downarrow$

2. $2\overline{)18}$ with quotient 9

3. Estimate: nine 23s in 187.

4. Check:
    $$\begin{array}{r} 23 \\ \times 9 \\ \hline 207 \end{array} \leftarrow \text{Too great.}$$

5. Try eight 23s.

6. Check: $\begin{array}{r} 23 \\ \times 8 \\ \hline 184 \end{array}$ ← Perfect.

7. $\begin{array}{r} 8\ R3 \\ 23\overline{)187} \\ -184 \\ \hline 3 \end{array}$

Example 2

1. $29\overline{)165}$

    ⇓

2. $2\overline{)16}^{\,8}$

3. Estimate: eight 29s in 165.

4. Check: $\begin{array}{r} 29 \\ \times 8 \\ \hline 232 \end{array}$ ← Way too great!

5. Maybe six 29s?

6. Check: $\begin{array}{r} 29 \\ \times 6 \\ \hline 174 \end{array}$ ← Slightly too great; five 29s should do it.

7. $\begin{array}{r} 5\ R20 \\ 29\overline{)165} \\ -145 \\ \hline 20 \end{array}$

Note that the estimate doesn't give an exact answer each time, but it can speed problems. First estimate the quotients, then divide.

Quick Quiz C

Directions: Complete the following problems.

1. $17\overline{)159}$ **4.** $45\overline{)389}$

2. $24\overline{)289}$ **5.** $53\overline{)627}$

3. $32\overline{)268}$ **6.** $23\overline{)864}$

More on Estimating Quotients

You may have noticed that some of your estimates for the quotients in the exercises were far away from the quotient you were looking for. That was especially true in example 2 in the last section. That's because of the way you were estimating. If the divisor was 29, you'd estimate by using the 2. Twenty-nine is really a lot closer to 30 than it is to 20. Estimating with 3 would have been better than using the 2.

The type of estimate you've been using is called "estimating by rounding down." The digit that you used to make the estimate was the tens digit less than the two-digit number you were dealing with. In other words, if you were dealing with 37, you'd round down to 30 and use the 3. If the divisor was 43, you'd round down to 40 and use the 4. Now, just as 43 is closer to 40 than to any other 10, 37 is closer to 40 than it is to 30. You're more likely to get an accurate estimate of the quotient if you used 4 rather than 3 as your estimated divisor. Choose the closer multiple of ten to the divisor to get a more accurate estimate. Look at the two models on the next page.

Estimating by Rounding Down

1. $87\overline{)243}$

    $\Downarrow$

2. $8\overline{)24}^{\,3}$ Estimate three 87s in 243.

3. Check: $\begin{array}{r} 87 \\ \times\ \ 3 \\ \hline 261 \end{array}$ ← Too great!

4. Try two 87s.

5. Check: $\begin{array}{r} 87 \\ \times\ \ 2 \\ \hline 174 \end{array}$ ← That works!

6. $\begin{array}{r} 2\ \text{R}69 \\ 87\overline{)243} \\ -174 \\ \hline 69 \end{array}$

Estimating by Rounding Up

1. $87\overline{)243}$

2. Close to 90. Estimate two 90s in 243.

3. $9\overline{)24}^{\,2}$

4. Check: $\begin{array}{r} 87 \\ \times\ \ 3 \\ \hline 174 \end{array}$ ← Looks good!

5. $\begin{array}{r} 2\ \text{R}69 \\ 87\overline{)243} \\ -\ 174 \\ \hline 69 \end{array}$

In this case, estimating by rounding up to the next decade (90) was a better way than rounding down. Sometimes it's better to round up, and sometimes it's better to round down. When the ones digit of the divisor is less than 5 (i.e., 0, 1, 2, 3, or 4), round down as you did in the last section. When the ones digit is 5 or greater, round up. The rounded tens' digit that you use to estimate the quotient is called **a trial divisor**.

Quick Quiz D

Directions: Name the trial divisor in each of the following problems. The first two have been done for you.

1. 32 is closer to 30, so the trial divisor would be 3.

2. 46 is closer to 50, so the trial divisor would be 5.

3. 29 is closer to_____, so the trial divisor would be _____.

4. 82 is closer to_____, so the trial divisor would be _____.

5. 73 is closer to_____, so the trial divisor would be _____.

6. 54 is closer to_____, so the trial divisor would be _____.

Now, try to apply the two different forms of estimating to some division exercises. Once you've found your trial divisor for a problem, that trial divisor will stay the same, no matter how many times you need to divide to complete that division. Perform these three steps for each:

1.   Estimate by rounding up or rounding down.

2.   Record your trial divisor.

3.   Divide.

Quick Quiz E

Directions: Find the trial divisor (T.D.).

1.
$$38\overline{)5943}$$
T.D. = _____

4.
$$62\overline{)9437}$$
T.D. = _____

2.
$$51\overline{)6782}$$
T.D. = _____

5.
$$55\overline{)7482}$$
T.D. = _____

3.
$$47\overline{)3895}$$
T.D. = _____

6.
$$38\overline{)4729}$$
T.D. = _____

You've now finished all four basic operations of arithmetic. These four operations are the basis for learning more math. Knowing how to add, subtract, multiply, and divide whole numbers will make learning about fractions and decimals much easier. Keep practicing your skills in the four operations so that the steps become automatic. Even doing one of each type of problem per day will help you.

Answers to Quick Quizzes

Answers to Quick Quiz A

1.
$$
\begin{array}{r}
18 \\
3\overline{)54} \\
-3\downarrow \\
\hline
24 \\
-24 \\
\hline
\end{array}
$$

4.
$$
\begin{array}{r}
23 \\
4\overline{)92} \\
-8\downarrow \\
\hline
12 \\
-12 \\
\hline
\end{array}
$$

2.
$$
\begin{array}{r}
16 \\
6\overline{)96} \\
-6\downarrow \\
\hline
36 \\
-36 \\
\hline
\end{array}
$$

5.
$$
\begin{array}{r}
19 \\
2\overline{)38} \\
-2\downarrow \\
\hline
18 \\
-18 \\
\hline
\end{array}
$$

3.
$$
\begin{array}{r}
17 \\
5\overline{)85} \\
-5\downarrow \\
\hline
35 \\
-35 \\
\hline
\end{array}
$$

6.
$$
\begin{array}{r}
14 \\
7\overline{)98} \\
-7\downarrow \\
\hline
28 \\
-28 \\
\hline
\end{array}
$$

Answers to Quick Quiz B

(It is correct to write the remainder either with an "R" or in fraction form.)

1. 68 R3
2. 65 R3
3. 206 R3
4. 122 R2
5. $47\frac{3}{4}$
6. 175

Answers to Quick Quiz C

1. 9 R6
2. 12 R1
3. 8 R12
4. 8 R38
5. 11 R44
6. 37 R13

Answers to Quick Quiz D

1. 30, 3
2. 50, 5
3. 30, 3
4. 80, 8
5. 70, 7
6. 50, 5

Answers to Quick Quiz E

1. 4; 156 R15
2. 5; 132 R50
3. 5; 82 R41
4. 6; 152 R13
5. 6; 136 R2
6. 4; 124 R17

Working with Fractions and Decimals

Understanding Fractions | 7

What Is a Fraction?

Fractions are one of the most poorly understood topics in math. They are used to represent many things, including:

- Part of a whole
- Part of a group of things
- Comparison or ratio
- Division
- Whole to be broken into parts

Part of a Whole

A fraction as a part of a whole assumes that there is one whole object, such as a cake or a paycheck. It also assumes you are referring to less than the entire object. The name of a fraction has two parts. The first is the number of equal parts that the whole is broken into. The second is the number of those parts being considered. Look at the following:

One of four equal parts: one-fourth = $\dfrac{1}{4}$

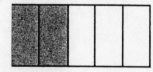

Two of five equal parts: two-fifths = $\dfrac{2}{5}$

Four of seven equal parts: four-sevenths = $\frac{4}{7}$

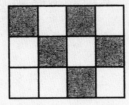

Five of twelve equal parts: five-twelfths = $\frac{5}{12}$

The bottom of a fraction tells the number of equal parts that the whole has been broken into. It is called the **denominator.** The top of the fraction is called the **numerator.** It tells the number of parts of the whole. In each of the samples above, the numerator tells how many parts are shaded.

Part of a Group

Sometimes you want to look at a fraction of a group of objects, instead of a single object. If you wanted to know how many (or 'what fraction') of the people at a movie are men, you would be looking at a part of a group. The following pictures show the meaning of fraction as a part of a group:

Two of five apples are shaded: $\frac{2}{5}$

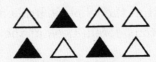

Three of eight triangles are shaded: $\frac{3}{8}$

$\frac{4}{7}$ are boys; $\frac{3}{7}$ are girls.

Math Essentials for the Pre-GED Student

$\frac{6}{11}$ are vertical; $\frac{5}{11}$ are horizontal.

Quick Quiz A

Directions: Name the fraction marked by the shaded portion in each diagram.

1.

6.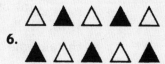

2.

7.

3.

8.

4.

5.

9.

Comparisons, Division, and Wholes to Be Broken

Fractions are often used to make comparisons. If you have $4 and Bill has $7, then you have $\frac{4}{7}$ as much money as Bill has. This way of using fractions is called **ratio.** You will learn more about ratios in Chapter 14.

Fractions are used in algebra to show division. The fraction line is the standard symbol used to show division on any computer keyboard: $\frac{8}{2}$ means 8 divided by 2. At the same time, $\frac{8}{2}$ also means 8 halves. In arithmetic, they mean the same thing, since 8 halves and 8 divided by 2 both equal 4.

Think of a fraction as any whole that is to be broken into smaller pieces. If you walk into a restaurant and order a piece of pie, you might notice that the pie was cut into eight equal parts. You wouldn't order "an eighth of pie." Instead, you order a "piece of pie," as if the eighth were a whole thing. If you weren't hungry enough to eat the whole piece, you might just eat half. You wouldn't say that you were eating a sixteenth of the original pie, you would say you ate "half a piece of pie." That's what is meant by saying that a fraction is any whole to be broken into smaller pieces.

Equivalent Fractions

Two fractions that are equal but have different names are called "equivalent fractions." Look at the diagram below:

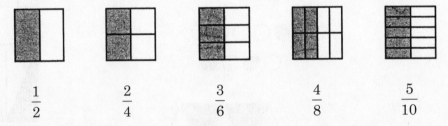

$$\frac{1}{2} \qquad \frac{2}{4} \qquad \frac{3}{6} \qquad \frac{4}{8} \qquad \frac{5}{10}$$

Each shaded fraction has a different name, as you can see from the name beneath each picture. But you can also see that the *size* of the piece shaded in each picture is the same. So, $\frac{1}{2}, \frac{2}{4}, \frac{3}{6}, \frac{4}{8}$, and $\frac{5}{10}$ are all **equivalent fractions.**

Quick Quiz B

Directions: Name the equivalent fractions.

There's an easier way to tell if fractions are equivalent. You can do this by finding common factors in the numerator and denominator of each.

Factors are numbers that multiply together to make another number. Two and four are factors of eight, for example. Common factors are factors that two numbers share. Six and eight have a common factor of 2.

Take another look at these equivalent fractions:

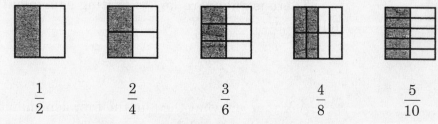

$$\frac{1}{2} \qquad \frac{2}{4} \qquad \frac{3}{6} \qquad \frac{4}{8} \qquad \frac{5}{10}$$

You can write the second fraction (the second box) like this:

$$\frac{2}{4} = \frac{2 \times 1}{2 \times 2} = \frac{2}{2} \times \frac{1}{2} \left(\text{but } \frac{2}{2} = 1, \text{ so} \right) = 1 \times \frac{1}{2} = \frac{1}{2}$$

Here's the third box on that line:

$$\frac{3}{6} = \frac{3 \times 1}{3 \times 2} = \frac{3}{3} \times \frac{1}{2} \left(\text{but } \frac{3}{3} = 1, \text{ so} \right) = 1 \times \frac{1}{2} = \frac{1}{2}$$

Here are the eighths (the fourth box):

$$\frac{4}{8} = \frac{4 \times 1}{4 \times 2} = \frac{4}{4} \times \frac{1}{2} \left(\text{but } \frac{4}{4} = 1, \text{ so} \right) = 1 \times \frac{1}{2} = \frac{1}{2}$$

And, finally, the tenths:

$$\frac{5}{10} = \frac{5 \times 1}{5 \times 2} = \frac{5}{5} \times \frac{1}{2} \left(\text{but } \frac{5}{5} = 1, \text{ so} \right) = 1 \times \frac{1}{2} = \frac{1}{2}$$

By finding the common factor that's contained in both the numerator and denominator of each fraction, you're able to write each fraction in **simplest form**. The simplest form for each of the fractions you just looked at turns out to be $\frac{1}{2}$. Simplest form is usually asked for when giving answers to fraction problems. Simplest form is explained again later in this section.

Any fraction that's written with the same number in the numerator as in the denominator (for example, $\frac{2}{2}$, $\frac{3}{3}$, $\frac{4}{4}$, $\frac{5}{5}$) has a value of 1. Two halves make one whole; three thirds make one whole, and so forth. Remember that fractions can also be thought of as division. That is, $\frac{2}{2}$ means 2 divided by 2, which is 1; $\frac{3}{3}$ means 3 divided by 3, which is 1.

There is one more key to writing equivalent fractions. Look at the following:

$$\frac{2}{3} = \frac{?}{9}$$

Ask yourself what the 3 in the first denominator was multiplied by to get the 9 of the second denominator. Then multiply the first numerator by the same amount. Note that $\therefore$ is the mathematical shorthand for "therefore."

$$\frac{2}{3 \times 3} = \frac{?}{9} \qquad \therefore \qquad \frac{2}{3} \times \frac{3}{3} = \frac{6}{9}$$

Notice that the first fraction has been multiplied by another name for 1: $\frac{3}{3}$.

Examine the two examples below:

Example 1

$$\frac{3}{8} = \frac{?}{24}$$

$$\frac{3}{8} \times \frac{}{3} = \frac{?}{24}$$

$$\frac{3}{8} \times \frac{3}{3} = \frac{?}{24}$$

$$\frac{3}{8} = \frac{9}{24}$$

Example 2

$$\frac{2}{3} = \frac{8}{?}$$

$$\frac{2}{3} \times \frac{4}{} = \frac{8}{?}$$

$$\frac{2}{3} \times \frac{4}{4} = \frac{8}{12}$$

$$\frac{2}{3} = \frac{8}{12}$$

Quick Quiz C

Directions: Complete the following to form equivalent fractions.

1. $\dfrac{1}{2} = \dfrac{}{4} = \dfrac{}{6} = \dfrac{}{8} = \dfrac{}{10} = \dfrac{}{12} = \dfrac{}{14} = \dfrac{}{16} = \dfrac{}{18} = \dfrac{}{20}$

2. $\dfrac{1}{3} = \dfrac{}{6} = \dfrac{}{9} = \dfrac{}{12} = \dfrac{}{15} = \dfrac{}{18} = \dfrac{}{21} = \dfrac{}{24} = \dfrac{}{27} = \dfrac{}{30}$

3. $\dfrac{2}{5} = \dfrac{}{10} = \dfrac{}{15} = \dfrac{}{20} = \dfrac{}{25} = \dfrac{}{30} = \dfrac{}{35} = \dfrac{}{40} = \dfrac{}{45} = \dfrac{}{50}$

4. $\dfrac{3}{7} = \dfrac{}{14} = \dfrac{}{21} = \dfrac{}{28} = \dfrac{}{35} = \dfrac{}{42} = \dfrac{}{49} = \dfrac{}{56} = \dfrac{}{63} = \dfrac{}{70}$

5. $\dfrac{5}{9} = \dfrac{}{18} = \dfrac{}{27} = \dfrac{}{36} = \dfrac{}{45} = \dfrac{}{54} = \dfrac{}{63} = \dfrac{}{72} = \dfrac{}{81} = \dfrac{}{90}$

6. $\dfrac{5}{8} = \dfrac{?}{40}$

7. $\dfrac{2}{3} = \dfrac{?}{36}$

8. $\dfrac{5}{9} = \dfrac{35}{?}$

9. $\dfrac{6}{13} = \dfrac{30}{?}$

10. $\dfrac{6}{11} = \dfrac{?}{66}$

Answers to Quick Quizzes

Answers to Quick Quiz A

1. $\dfrac{1}{4}$

2. $\dfrac{3}{10}$

3. $\dfrac{2}{3}$

4. $\dfrac{4}{9}$

5. $\dfrac{2}{5}$

6. $\dfrac{5}{10}$ or $\dfrac{1}{2}$

7. $\dfrac{7}{16}$

8. $\dfrac{8}{15}$

9. $\dfrac{3}{8}$

Answers to Quick Quiz B

1. $\dfrac{1}{3}, \dfrac{2}{6}, \dfrac{3}{9}, \dfrac{4}{12}$

2. $\dfrac{1}{4}, \dfrac{2}{8}, \dfrac{4}{16}, \dfrac{3}{12}$

3. $\dfrac{2}{5}, \dfrac{4}{10}, \dfrac{6}{15}, \dfrac{8}{20}$

Answers to Quick Quiz C

1. 2, 3, 4, 5, 6, 7, 8, 9, 10

2. 2, 3, 4, 5, 6, 7, 8, 9, 10

3. 4, 6, 8, 10, 12, 14, 16, 18, 20

4. 6, 9, 12, 15, 18, 21, 24, 27, 30

5. 10, 15, 20, 25, 30, 35, 40, 45, 50

6. 25

7. 24

8. 63

9. 65

10. 36

Add and Subtract Fractions | 8

Adding and Subtracting Fractions

Fractions, like all numbers, can be added, subtracted, multiplied, and divided. This chapter covers both adding and subtracting fractions, since the rules for both are very similar. In fact, there is really only one:

Fractions may be added or subtracted if they have like denominators.

Fractions with Like Denominators

Remember that a fraction's denominator is the number on the bottom. It names the number of parts into which the whole object or group has been separated. If two fractions have the same number on the bottom, they have **like denominators.** It's important to remember that the denominator names the *size* of the parts that are being dealt with. For example, if an object is divided into eighths, there will be twice as many parts as there would be if the same object were divided into fourths. Each eighth, however, would be half the size of each fourth.

Fourths $\frac{1}{4}$ $\frac{1}{8}$

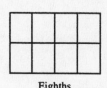

Eighths

For objects of the same size whole, the more parts there are, the smaller each part is. The following diagram shows the addition of $\frac{1}{5}$ and $\frac{2}{5}$:

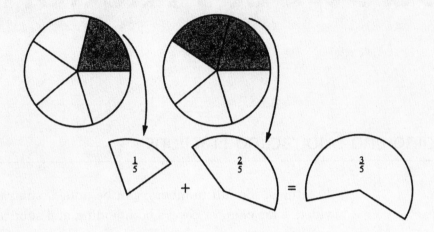

Notice that the numerators (top numbers in the fractions) tell the number of parts being considered. For example, the number 1 names the first amount of fifths, and the number 2 names the second amount of fifths. Adding one and two gives three, so adding $\frac{1}{5}$ and $\frac{2}{5}$ gives $\frac{3}{5}$. Notice that you started with fifths and ended with fifths—*the denominators do not change. Only the numerators are added.* Here's another example:

$$\frac{1}{4} \quad + \quad \frac{2}{4} \quad = \quad \frac{3}{4}$$

Subtracting fractional numbers works exactly the same way as addition, except that the numerators are subtracted rather than added:

$$\frac{4}{4} \quad - \quad \frac{1}{4} \quad = \quad \frac{3}{4}$$

> **When adding fractions, only the numerators are added. The denominators represent the size of the pieces being added, and they stay the same in the answer.**

Quick Quiz A

Directions: Complete the fractional additions and subtractions below. Watch the signs, so that you know whether to add or subtract.

1. $\dfrac{2}{7} + \dfrac{3}{7} =$ ___

2. $\dfrac{4}{9} + \dfrac{3}{9} =$ ___

3. $\dfrac{7}{12} - \dfrac{2}{12} =$ ___

4. $\dfrac{11}{20} - \dfrac{8}{20} =$ ___

5. $\dfrac{9}{17} + \dfrac{6}{17} =$ ___

6. $\dfrac{8}{21} + \dfrac{9}{21} =$ ___

7. $\dfrac{4}{11} + \dfrac{5}{11} =$ ___

8. $\dfrac{11}{15} - \dfrac{7}{15} =$ ___

9. $\dfrac{6}{14} + \dfrac{5}{14} =$ ___

10. $\dfrac{13}{16} - \dfrac{8}{16} =$ ___

Greatest Common Factor

Look at this set of numbers: {9, 12, 18, 24}. All of the numbers in the set are divisible by 1. Divisible means "can be divided exactly by." All of the numbers in the set are also divisible by 3. There are no other numbers that 9, 12, 18, and 24, as a set, are divisible by. Three is the greatest number by that they are divisible. In other words, 3 is the **greatest common factor (GCF)** of 9, 12, 18, and 24.

The Greatest Common Factor (GCF) is the greatest factor that a set of numbers all share.

Suppose you're asked to find the greatest common factor of {10, 20, 30, 45}. You know that 1 is a factor of each number in the set. Five is another factor of each number. You can tell that each is divisible by 5 since each number ends in 0 or 5. Ten perfectly divides each number in the set except the last, so it is not a factor of all the numbers. There are no other factors of 10, so you are done checking since the GCF has to be a factor of 10. This means that the greatest common factor of the four numbers is 5.

Another way to find the greatest common factor is to make a list of all the factors of each number. Make a list of all the factors of the two numbers, and then look for the greatest number that is in both lists.

Remember that if all the numbers are even, your GCF will be at least 2 since all even numbers are divisible by 2.

The GCF is the best way to put a fraction into simplest form. You should answer arithmetic problems involving fractions in simplest form. Find the GCF of the numerator and denominator. Divide the numerator and denominator by the GCF and your fraction is in simplest form.

Quick Quiz B

Directions: Find the greatest common factor of each of the following sets.

1. 14, 21, 28   **6.** 24, 36

2. 6, 12, 15   **7.** 45, 60

3. 8, 12, 20   **8.** 12, 17

4. 25, 40   **9.** 12, 42

5. 18, 30   **10.** 16, 24, 32

Least Common Multiple

The **least common multiple** (LCM) is the least multiple that the set of numbers all share. When you understand the basics about least common multiples (LCM), it makes working with fractions much easier. You'll see how LCM is used in the next section. Many people get the GCF and LCM confused. It's very important to understand the difference between factors and multiples. Factors are numbers that you multiply together to get the product. Multiples, on the other hand, are what you get when you skip count by a given number. Zero can't be the LCM. The greatest LCM possible when you have two numbers is the product of the two numbers. Many times the LCM is much less than that product, so multiplying the two numbers together is not a good shortcut. Here is an example of how to find the LCM:

Take two numbers: 2 and 4. Now look at some of the multiples of 2 and of 4:

- **Multiples of 2:** 2, 4, 6, 8, 10, 12, 14, 16, 18, 20,…
- **Multiples of 4:** 4, 8, 12, 16, 20,…

Now, circle the common multiples of 2 and 4—that is, the numbers that appear in both sets of multiples. You should have circled 4, 8, 12, 16, and 20. Those are all common multiples of 2 and 4. Since the LCM is the least common, the LCM for 2 and 4 is 4.

The **least common multiple** (LCM) is the least multiple that a set of numbers all share. Zero cannot be the LCM.

Sometimes, the LCM is the greater of the numbers in the given set. For example, the LCM of 2 and 6 is 6.

Quick Quiz C

Directions: List the first 10 multiples for each of the following pairs of numbers.

1. 3 _____   **4.** 8 _____

    4 _____   4 _____

2. 5 _____   **5.** 8 _____

    3 _____   12 _____

3. 6 _____   **6.** 9 _____

    8 _____   8 _____

Directions: Now name the LCM for each of the pairs of numbers above.

7. _____   **10.** _____

8. _____   **11.** _____

9. _____   **12.** _____

Quick Quiz D

Directions: Find the LCMs for the following pairs of numbers.

1. 7, 11   **6.** 8, 2

2. 8, 3   **7.** 5, 17

3. 5, 4   **8.** 2, 18

4. 4, 6   **9.** 3, 20

5. 9, 12   **10.** 18, 4

Adding and Subtracting Using Equivalent Fractions

You first looked at adding and subtracting fractions with like denominators. But often, you'll have to add or subtract fractions with different denominators. Follow along with this example:

Example

Mr. Anderson painted $\frac{3}{8}$ of his garage on Tuesday. Mrs. Anderson then painted $\frac{1}{6}$ on Wednesday. How much of the garage was painted?

Since one person painted a part of the garage, and then the other person did another part of the same job, you have to add to find out how much of the job was done altogether: $\frac{3}{8} + \frac{1}{6} = ?$ But this addition can't be done the way it looks now. The denominators are not the same, so you can't add until you can create equivalent fractions that have the same denominators.

Look at the denominators of the two fractions: $\frac{}{8} + \frac{}{6}$

They're 8 and 6. Their least common multiple (LCM) is 24. Now you can write equivalent fractions for $\frac{3}{8}$ and $\frac{1}{6}$ using 24 as the least common denominator (LCD). Once you write the equivalent fractions, they can be added to find the sum:

$$\frac{3}{8} \times \frac{3}{3} = \frac{9}{24}$$
$$+\frac{1}{6} \times \frac{4}{4} = \frac{4}{24}$$
$$\frac{13}{24}$$

Here are the steps for adding fractions with unlike denominators:

1. **Find** the LCM of the denominators.

2. **Make** the LCM the least common denominator to use for writing equivalent fractions.

3. **Write** equivalent fractions with common denominators.

4. **Add** the equivalent fractions to find the sum.

The two examples below show two different styles of adding fractions. Decide which style works best for you, and then stick with it.

Example 1

$$\frac{1}{3} + \frac{2}{5} = ?$$

LCM for 3 and 5 = 15   LCD = 15ths

Write equivalent fractions and add:

$$\frac{1}{3} = \frac{3}{15}$$
$$+\frac{2}{5} = \frac{6}{15}$$
$$\frac{9}{15} \text{ or } \frac{3}{5}$$

Example 2

$$\frac{3}{6} + \frac{1}{4} = ?$$

LCM for 6 and 4 = 12   LCD = 12ths

Write equivalent fractions and add:

$$\frac{}{12} + \frac{}{12} = \frac{}{12}$$
$$\frac{6}{12} + \frac{3}{12} = \frac{9}{12} \text{ or } \frac{3}{4}$$

Subtraction of fractional numbers is done the same way as addition of fractional numbers. Find common denominators for the two fractions and, once the denominators are the same, simply subtract the numerators.

Here are the steps for adding fractions with unlike denominators:

1. **Find** the LCM of the denominators.

2. **Make** the LCM the least common denominator to use for writing equivalent fractions.

3. **Write** equivalent fractions with common denominators.

4. **Subtract** the equivalent fractions to find the sum.

Quick Quiz E

Directions: Add or subtract the following fractions.

1. $\dfrac{1}{3} + \dfrac{2}{4} = ?$

2. $\dfrac{1}{5} + \dfrac{1}{3} = ?$

3. $\dfrac{5}{8} - \dfrac{2}{5} = ?$

4. $\dfrac{11}{12} - \dfrac{5}{6} = ?$

5. $\dfrac{5}{8} - \dfrac{5}{12} = ?$

6. $\dfrac{3}{14} + \dfrac{5}{7} = ?$

7. $\dfrac{1}{11} + \dfrac{1}{2} = ?$

8. $\dfrac{3}{5} - \dfrac{4}{7} = ?$

9. $\dfrac{11}{15} - \dfrac{1}{4} = ?$

10. $\dfrac{4}{9} + \dfrac{2}{5} = ?$

Expressing Fractions in Simplest Form

You've already seen that the same fraction can be written in many ways (equivalent fractions). Often, including on the GED test, you must write a fraction in its **simplest form**. Putting a fraction into simplest form means that you write it with the least numerator and denominator possible. Here is an example:

$\frac{24}{32}$ can be written as an equivalent fraction by dividing the numerator and the denominator by 2. When you do this, you get $\frac{12}{16}$. But this fraction can have its numerator and denominator divided by 2 again, to get $\frac{6}{8}$. Since 2 is a factor of both 6 and 8, $\frac{6}{8}$ still isn't in simplest form. Dividing both numerator and denominator by 2 yet again, we get $\frac{3}{4}$. There is no number, except for 1, that can divide both 3 and 4 exactly. That means that $\frac{3}{4}$ is the simplest form of $\frac{24}{32}$.

The method you just used meant finding a common factor in the numerator and denominator, and then dividing both by that factor. The process was done over and over, until no common factor of both the numerator and denominator remained. This method works fine, but may be very time-consuming. An easier way to simplify fractions is to use the GCF.

Here's the original fraction again: $\frac{24}{32}$. What is the GCF for 24 and 32?

The greatest common factor of 24 and 32 which is 8. Eight is the greatest number by which both 24 and 32 can be divided exactly. Now, divide both numerator and denominator by the GCF:

$$\frac{24 \div 8}{32 \div 8} = \frac{3}{4}$$

Remember, when a number is divided by 1 (expressed as $\frac{8}{8}$ in this case), its value does not change. That means that $\frac{3}{4}$ is equivalent, or equal, to $\frac{24}{32}$ and is that fraction's value in simplest form.

To write a fraction in simplest form, divide the numerator and denominator by the greatest common factor (GCF) of its numerator and denominator.

Quick Quiz F

Directions: Express the following fractions in simplest form.

1. $\dfrac{10}{12}$

2. $\dfrac{15}{30}$

3. $\dfrac{18}{24}$

4. $\dfrac{24}{32}$

5. $\dfrac{9}{15}$

6. $\dfrac{12}{18}$

7. $\dfrac{25}{30}$

8. $\dfrac{56}{64}$

9. $\dfrac{50}{60}$

10. $\dfrac{32}{36}$

The answers to fraction problems are usually expressed in simplest form. Some books also refer to expressing fractions in simplest form as "reducing." "Simplest form" is a better term since you aren't really making the fraction less. The numbers in the fraction may look less, but the value of the fraction stays the same. When you put a fraction in simplest form, you're making an equivalent fraction, not a lesser or "reduced" fraction.

Fractional answers on the GED exam are almost always written in simplest form. Practice expressing the answers to any fraction problems in that form.

Quick Quiz G

Directions: Solve and express your answers in simplest form.

1. $\dfrac{3}{9} + \dfrac{2}{6} = $ _____

2. $\dfrac{1}{2} + \dfrac{1}{6} = $ _____

3. $\dfrac{11}{12} - \dfrac{1}{4} = $ _____

4. $\dfrac{7}{18} - \dfrac{1}{6} = $ _____

5. $\dfrac{1}{5} + \dfrac{6}{15} = $ _____

6. $\dfrac{17}{20} - \dfrac{1}{4} = $ _____

7. $\dfrac{23}{24} - \dfrac{1}{8} = $ _____

8. $\dfrac{2}{7} + \dfrac{1}{3} = $ _____

9. $\dfrac{3}{5} - \dfrac{4}{15} = $ _____

10. $\dfrac{6}{9} - \dfrac{1}{4} = $ _____

Fractions Greater than One

A number consisting of a whole number and a fraction is known as a **mixed number**. The number 2 is a whole number. $\frac{1}{2}$ is a fraction. $2\frac{1}{2}$ (read as "two and one half") is a mixed number. Any fraction whose numerator is greater than its denominator can be written as a whole or as a mixed number. The change is done by dividing the numerator by the denominator. Check out the examples below:

Example 1

$$\frac{17}{2}$$
$$\downarrow$$
$$2\overline{)17}$$
$$\downarrow$$
$$8\frac{1}{2}$$

Example 2

$$\frac{30}{5}$$
$$\downarrow$$
$$5\overline{)30}$$
$$\downarrow$$
$$6$$

Adding with Mixed Numbers

Since mixed numbers have both a whole number part and a fraction part, the way you add them is to treat each part separately.

- First, add the fractions, making sure to have common denominators.

- It is important to add the fractions before the whole numbers. If you get a mixed number when you add the fractions, you can add the whole number portion of it to the other whole numbers.

- Then, add the whole numbers.

Here are some examples:

Example 1

$$3\frac{1}{8} \ + \ 4\frac{3}{8}$$

$$\downarrow$$

$$3\frac{1}{8}$$

$$+4\frac{3}{8}$$

$$\overline{\frac{4}{8}}$$ First, add the fractions.

$$\downarrow$$

$$3\frac{1}{8}$$

$$+4\frac{3}{8}$$ Next, add the whole numbers.

$$\overline{7\frac{4}{8}} \ \to \ 7\frac{1}{2}$$

Example 2

$$5\frac{3}{4} \ + \ 3\frac{3}{4}$$

$$\downarrow$$

$$5\frac{3}{4}$$

$$+3\frac{3}{4}$$

$$\overline{\frac{6}{4}} \ \to \ 1\frac{1}{2}$$ First, add the fractions.

Add the whole number, 1, to the
other whole numbers, 5 and 3.

$$\overset{1}{5}\frac{3}{4}$$

$$+3\frac{3}{4}$$

$$\overline{9\frac{1}{2}}$$ $\leftarrow$ Remember to add the fraction
to the final result.

Example 3

$$5\frac{1}{2} \rightarrow 5\frac{6}{12} \rightarrow 5\frac{6}{12}$$

$$+3\frac{5}{12} \rightarrow +3\frac{5}{12} \rightarrow +3\frac{5}{12}$$

$$\frac{11}{12} \qquad 8\frac{11}{12}$$

Note that the fractions must have like denominators to be added.

Example 4

$$3\frac{9}{10} \rightarrow 3\frac{18}{20} \rightarrow 3\frac{18}{20} \rightarrow {}^{1}3\frac{18}{20} \rightarrow {}^{1}3\frac{18}{20}$$

$$+4\frac{17}{20} \rightarrow +4\frac{17}{20} \rightarrow +4\frac{17}{20} \rightarrow +4\frac{17}{20} \rightarrow +4\frac{17}{20}$$

$$\frac{35}{20} = 1\frac{3}{4} \qquad\qquad \frac{3}{4} \qquad 8\frac{3}{4}$$

Steps for Adding Mixed Numbers

1. If the denominators are the same, skip to step 4. If the denominators are not the same, find the LCM of the denominators.

2. Make the LCM the least common denominator to use for writing equivalent fractions.

3. Write equivalent fractions with common denominators.

4. Add the equivalent fractions. If their sum is more than 1, rename the fraction as a mixed number, and move the whole number into the column with the other whole numbers.

5. Add the whole numbers.

6. Write the fraction part of the mixed number in simplest form.

Quick Quiz H

Directions: Add and express the sum as a mixed number in simplest form.

1. $4\dfrac{3}{5}$
   $+2\dfrac{4}{5}$

6. $4\dfrac{3}{4}$
   $+3\dfrac{1}{2}$

2. $4\dfrac{2}{8}$
   $+3\dfrac{3}{8}$

7. $5\dfrac{3}{7}$
   $+4\dfrac{5}{8}$

3. $5\dfrac{3}{4}$
   $+5\dfrac{1}{4}$

8. $2\dfrac{1}{8}$
   $+6\dfrac{5}{6}$

4. $4\dfrac{5}{6}$
   $+5\dfrac{5}{6}$

9. $6\dfrac{1}{3}$
   $+5\dfrac{1}{4}$

5. $3\dfrac{1}{8}$
   $+2\dfrac{3}{16}$

10. $5\dfrac{1}{3}$
    $+2\dfrac{3}{8}$

Subtracting with Mixed Numbers

Subtracting mixed numbers is very similar to adding them. Try the following problems.

Quick Quiz I

Directions: Subtract the fractions first, and then the whole numbers.

1.
$$7\frac{5}{9}$$
$$-\,2\frac{3}{9}$$

2.
$$8\frac{4}{5}$$
$$-\,2\frac{1}{3}$$

3.
$$9\frac{3}{4}$$
$$-\,4\frac{1}{3}$$

4.
$$7\frac{11}{12}$$
$$-\,3\frac{1}{2}$$

5.
$$8\frac{4}{5}$$
$$-\,3\frac{1}{3}$$

6.
$$10\frac{7}{8}$$
$$-\,5\frac{2}{3}$$

Not all subtractions of fractions, however, are this easy. Look at the following example:

Example:
$$7\frac{1}{4}$$
$$-\,5\frac{3}{4}$$

Notice that since $\frac{3}{4}$ is greater than $\frac{1}{4}$, it can't be subtracted from it. (At least, it can't be subtracted from it to get a positive value, which is what you need here.)

To be able to subtract one fraction from the other, you must make the first fraction greater. Do this by regrouping from the whole numbers. Re-name 1 from the 7 as a fraction, $\frac{4}{4}$.

$$
7\frac{1}{4} \qquad \rightarrow \qquad 6 + \frac{4}{4} + \frac{1}{4} \qquad \rightarrow \qquad 6\frac{5}{4}
$$
$$
-5\frac{3}{4} \qquad\qquad\qquad\qquad\qquad\qquad\qquad -5\frac{3}{4}
$$

Now, since there's a greater fraction on top than on the bottom, you can subtract:

$$
6\frac{5}{4}
$$
$$
-5\frac{3}{4}
$$
$$
\overline{1\frac{2}{4}} \;=\; 1\frac{1}{2}
$$

Quick Quiz J

Directions: Following the example above as a guide, subtract the following and express your answers in simplest form.

1.
$$
\begin{array}{c|c|c}
7\frac{3}{8} & 6+\frac{8}{8}+\frac{3}{8} & 6\frac{11}{8} \\
-3\frac{5}{8} & -3\frac{5}{8} & -3\frac{5}{8} \\
\hline
& & 3\frac{6}{8} = \underline{}
\end{array}
$$

4.
$$
8\frac{1}{3}
$$
$$
-5\frac{2}{3}
$$

2.
$$
8\frac{3}{5}
$$
$$
-4\frac{4}{5}
$$

5.
$$
5\frac{7}{16}
$$
$$
-2\frac{11}{16}
$$

3.
$$
9\frac{1}{4}
$$
$$
-3\frac{3}{4}
$$

6.
$$
7\frac{1}{9}
$$
$$
-4\frac{7}{9}
$$

It's also possible to have different denominators in the fraction parts of mixed numbers. The next examples put together all of the steps that you may need in a mixed number subtraction.

Example 1

$$8\frac{2}{3} \quad \rightarrow \quad 8\frac{8}{12} \quad \rightarrow \quad 7\frac{12}{12} \quad + \quad \frac{8}{12} \quad \rightarrow \quad 7\frac{20}{12}$$

$$-3\frac{3}{4} \quad \rightarrow \quad -3\frac{9}{12} \quad \rightarrow \quad\quad \rightarrow \quad\quad \rightarrow \quad -3\frac{9}{12}$$

$$4\frac{11}{12}$$

Example 2

$$9\frac{2}{5}\;\overset{\cdot\,4}{\rightarrow} \quad 9\frac{8}{20} \quad \rightarrow \quad 8\frac{20}{20} \quad + \quad \frac{8}{20} \quad \rightarrow \quad 8\frac{28}{20}$$

$$-5\frac{3}{4}\;\overset{\cdot\,5}{\rightarrow} \quad -5\frac{15}{20} \quad \rightarrow \quad \rightarrow \quad \rightarrow \quad \rightarrow \quad \rightarrow \quad -5\frac{15}{20}$$

$$3\frac{13}{20}$$

Steps for Subtracting Mixed Numbers

1. If the denominators are the same, skip to step 4. If the denominators are not the same, find the LCM of the denominators.

2. Make the LCM the least common denominator to use for writing equivalent fractions.

3. Write equivalent fractions with common denominators.

4. Subtract the equivalent fractions. If the bottom fraction is larger than the top fraction, rename a whole and add it to the top fraction.

5. Subtract the whole numbers.

6. Write the fraction part of the mixed number in lowest terms.

Quick Quiz K

Directions: Solve the following mixed number subtractions.

1.
$$\begin{array}{r} 4\frac{3}{5} \\ -2\frac{4}{5} \\ \hline \end{array}$$

4.
$$\begin{array}{r} 6\frac{1}{16} \\ -2\frac{3}{8} \\ \hline \end{array}$$

2.
$$\begin{array}{r} 5\frac{1}{3} \\ -2\frac{3}{8} \\ \hline \end{array}$$

5.
$$\begin{array}{r} 9\frac{1}{4} \\ -7\frac{5}{6} \\ \hline \end{array}$$

3.
$$\begin{array}{r} 4\frac{2}{7} \\ -3\frac{7}{8} \\ \hline \end{array}$$

6.
$$\begin{array}{r} 10\frac{1}{3} \\ -7\frac{2}{3} \\ \hline \end{array}$$

You survived adding and subtracting fractions! The most important thing to remember from this chapter is that you must have common denominators to add and subtract fractions. Also remember that only the numerators get added or subtracted; the denominators stay the same. In the next chapter, you'll learn how to multiply and divide fractions. Many people find that easier than adding and subtracting since you don't need common denominators.

Answers to Quick Quizzes

Answers to Quick Quiz A

1. $\dfrac{5}{7}$

2. $\dfrac{7}{9}$

3. $\dfrac{5}{12}$

4. $\dfrac{3}{20}$

5. $\dfrac{15}{17}$

6. $\dfrac{17}{21}$

7. $\dfrac{9}{11}$

8. $\dfrac{4}{15}$

9. $\dfrac{11}{14}$

10. $\dfrac{5}{16}$

Answers to Quick Quiz B

1. 7

2. 3

3. 4

4. 5

5. 6

6. 12

7. 15

8. 1

9. 6

10. 8

Answers to Quick Quiz C

1. 3, 6, 9, 12, 15, 18, 21, 24, 27, 30
4, 8, 12, 16, 20, 24, 28, 32, 36, 40

2. 5, 10, 15, 20, 25, 30, 35, 40, 45, 50
3, 6, 9, 12, 15, 18, 21, 24, 27, 30

3. 6, 12, 18, 24, 30, 36, 42, 48, 54, 60
8, 16, 24, 32, 40, 48, 56, 64, 72, 80

4. 8, 16, 24, 32, 40, 48, 56, 64, 72, 80
4, 8, 12, 16, 20, 24, 28, 32, 36, 40

5. 8, 16, 24, 32, 40, 48, 56, 64, 72, 80
12, 24, 36, 48, 60, 72, 84, 96, 108, 120

6. 9, 18, 27, 36, 45, 54, 63, 72, 81, 90
8, 16, 24, 32, 40, 48, 56, 64, 72, 80

7. 12

8. 15

9. 24

10. 8

11. 24

12. 72

Answers to Quick Quiz D

1. 77
2. 24
3. 20
4. 12
5. 36

6. 8
7 85
8. 18
9. 60
10. 36

Answers to Quick Quiz E

1. $\frac{10}{12}$ or $\frac{5}{6}$
2. $\frac{8}{15}$
3. $\frac{9}{40}$
4. $\frac{1}{12}$
5. $\frac{5}{24}$

6. $\frac{13}{14}$
7. $\frac{13}{22}$
8. $\frac{1}{35}$
9. $\frac{29}{60}$
10. $\frac{38}{45}$

Answers to Quick Quiz F

1. $\frac{5}{6}$
2. $\frac{1}{2}$
3. $\frac{3}{4}$
4. $\frac{3}{4}$
5. $\frac{3}{5}$

6. $\frac{2}{3}$
7. $\frac{5}{6}$
8. $\frac{7}{8}$
9. $\frac{5}{6}$
10. $\frac{8}{9}$

Answers to Quick Quiz G

1. $\dfrac{2}{3}$

2. $\dfrac{2}{3}$

3. $\dfrac{2}{3}$

4. $\dfrac{2}{9}$

5. $\dfrac{3}{5}$

6. $\dfrac{3}{5}$

7. $\dfrac{5}{6}$

8. $\dfrac{13}{21}$

9. $\dfrac{1}{3}$

10. $\dfrac{5}{12}$

Answers to Quick Quiz H

1. $7\dfrac{2}{5}$

2. $7\dfrac{5}{8}$

3. 11

4. $10\dfrac{2}{3}$

5. $5\dfrac{5}{16}$

6. $8\dfrac{1}{4}$

7. $10\dfrac{3}{56}$

8. $8\dfrac{23}{24}$

9. $11\dfrac{7}{12}$

10. $7\dfrac{17}{24}$

Answers to Quick Quiz I

1. $5\dfrac{2}{9}$

2. $6\dfrac{7}{15}$

3. $5\dfrac{5}{12}$

4. $4\dfrac{5}{12}$

5. $5\dfrac{7}{15}$

6. $5\dfrac{5}{24}$

Answers to Quick Quiz J

1. $3\dfrac{3}{4}$

2. $3\dfrac{4}{5}$

3. $5\dfrac{1}{2}$

4. $2\dfrac{2}{3}$

5. $2\dfrac{3}{4}$

6. $2\dfrac{1}{3}$

Answers to Quick Quiz K

1. $1\dfrac{4}{5}$

2. $2\dfrac{23}{24}$

3. $\dfrac{23}{56}$

4. $3\dfrac{11}{16}$

5. $1\dfrac{5}{12}$

6. $2\dfrac{2}{3}$

Multiplying and Dividing Fractions | 9

Multiplying Fractions

Multiplying fractions seems a lot like multiplying whole numbers at first because it's done in almost the same way. When whole numbers are multiplied together, the product (answer) is greater than those numbers. When fractional numbers are multiplied together, however, the product generally becomes less than either of the fractions. To see why, substitute the word "of" for the multiplication sign in a whole number. Then do the same thing in a fractional one:

3×4 • • • •   Look at the four. Change the "×" to "of."

$\downarrow$ $\downarrow$

3 of 4 • • • •

           • • • •   Here are three of them.

           • • • •

3 4s $= 12$ Three fours make twelve.

Here is how it works with fractional numbers:

$\dfrac{1}{2} \times \dfrac{1}{2}$ Look at the second one half. Change the "×" to "of."

$\dfrac{1}{2}$ of $\dfrac{1}{2}$ Here is one half of one half.

$\dfrac{1}{2}$ of $\dfrac{1}{2} = \dfrac{1}{4}$ Half of one half is one fourth.

As you can see from the drawing, multiplying fractions can be thought of as taking a part of a part of something. When you take a part of a part of something, the resulting part will be less than the original part.

Multiplying fractions is very simple. Multiply numerator by numerator and denominator by denominator. You don't need a common denominator before you multiply. Here is an example:

$$\frac{2}{3} \times \frac{5}{7} = \frac{2 \times 5}{3 \times 7} = \frac{10}{21}$$

Quick Quiz A

Directions: Multiply the following, and express the products (answers) in simplest form.

1. $\frac{4}{5} \times \frac{5}{8} = $ _____

5. $\frac{5}{6} \times \frac{3}{10} = $ _____

2. $\frac{1}{3} \times \frac{3}{8} = $ _____

6. $\frac{3}{8} \times \frac{4}{5} = $ _____

3. $\frac{4}{9} \times \frac{3}{7} = $ _____

7. $\frac{4}{7} \times \frac{21}{16} = $ _____

4. $\frac{4}{7} \times \frac{5}{8} = $ _____

8. $\frac{6}{13} \times \frac{26}{36} = $ _____

Dividing Common Factors

Dividing by common factors is a way to make it easier to multiply two fractions and express the result in simplest form. If you divide by common factors every place it's possible before you multiply, then your answer should be in simplest form.

If you are trying to express a fraction in simplest form, you look for the greatest common factor in the numerator and the denominator. Then you divide the numerator and denominator by that number. When fractions are being multiplied together, you can divide common factors out of any numerator-denominator pair, even if they are not part of the same fraction. Here is how it works:

$$\frac{3}{8} \times \frac{4}{5} \quad \rightarrow \quad \frac{3}{\underset{2}{8}} \times \frac{\overset{1}{4}}{5} \quad \rightarrow \quad \frac{3}{2} \times \frac{1}{5} = \frac{3}{10}$$

Both 4 and 8 could be divided by the GCF of 4. Four divided by 4 is 1, and 8 divided by 4 is 2. Now multiply the new fractions together. Your answer is already in simplest form.

Here's another example:

$$\frac{3}{7} \times \frac{21}{6}$$

$$\downarrow$$

$$\overset{1}{\frac{3}{7}} \times \frac{21}{\underset{2}{6}}$$ 3 is the GCF for 3 and 6 . . .

$$\downarrow$$

$$\frac{1}{\underset{1}{7}} \times \frac{\overset{3}{21}}{2}$$ 7 is the GCF for 7 and 21.

$$\downarrow$$

$$\frac{1}{1} \times \frac{3}{2} = \frac{3}{2} = 1\frac{1}{2}$$

To multiply fractions, multiply the numerators together and then multiply the denominators together. Divide by common factors before multiplying whenever possible, so that your answers will be in simplest form.

Divide by common factors before multiplying whenever possible. If your product isn't in simplest form, check back to see what else you could have divided by.

Quick Quiz B

Directions: Multiply the following fractions.

1. $\frac{4}{9} \times \frac{3}{4} =$ _____

2. $\frac{7}{18} \times \frac{9}{14} =$ _____

3. $\frac{10}{24} \times \frac{8}{15} =$ _____

4. $\frac{12}{17} \times \frac{1}{8} =$ _____

5. $\frac{5}{9} \times \frac{3}{8} =$ _____

6. $\frac{5}{11} \times \frac{3}{10} =$ _____

7. $\frac{17}{48} \times \frac{24}{34} =$ _____

8. $\frac{9}{14} \times \frac{21}{36} =$ _____

9. $\frac{5}{2} \times \frac{5}{9} \times \frac{18}{25} =$ _____

10. $\frac{3}{6} \times \frac{3}{2} \times \frac{4}{9} =$ _____

Dividing Fractions

Reciprocals

Dividing fractions uses the fact that division and multiplication are **reciprocal operations**. To understand what that means, first look at the meaning of **reciprocals.** The reciprocal of a number is the number you multiply it by to get a product of one. For example:

The reciprocal of 2 is $\dfrac{1}{2}$, since $2 \times \dfrac{1}{2} = 1$.

The reciprocal of $\dfrac{1}{4}$ is 4, since $\dfrac{1}{4} \times 4 = 1$.

The reciprocal of $\dfrac{3}{4}$ is $\dfrac{4}{3}$, since $\dfrac{3}{4} \times \dfrac{4}{3} = 1$.

Quick Quiz C

Directions: Name the reciprocal of the following.

1. 5

2. 8

3. 27

4. $\dfrac{1}{9}$

5. $\dfrac{1}{27}$

6. $\dfrac{1}{345}$

7. $\dfrac{2}{3}$

8. $\dfrac{8}{83}$

9. $\dfrac{17}{69}$

10. $\dfrac{123}{517}$

All division problems can be solved by multiplying. Multiply the dividend (the number being divided) by the reciprocal of the divisor (the number you are dividing by). Take a look at the following two division examples. Each has been rewritten as a multiplication by the reciprocal of the divisor.

Example 1

$$8 \div 2$$
$$\downarrow$$
$$8 \times \dfrac{1}{2}$$
$$\downarrow$$
$$\dfrac{8}{1} \times \dfrac{1}{2} = \dfrac{8}{2} = 4$$

Example 2

$$3\overline{)24}$$

$$\downarrow$$

$$24 \div 3$$

$$\downarrow$$

$$24 \times \frac{1}{3}$$

$$\downarrow$$

$$\frac{24}{1} \times \frac{1}{3} = \frac{24}{3} = 8$$

Notice in these examples that it's always the number being divided *by* whose reciprocal is used.

Quick Quiz D

Directions: Change each to a reciprocal multiplication and solve.

1. $18 \div 3 = \dfrac{18}{1} \times \square = \square$

2. $5\overline{)35} = 35 \div 5 = \dfrac{35}{1} \times \square = \square$

3. $15 \div 5 = \dfrac{15}{1} \times \square = \square$

4. $16 \div 4 = \dfrac{16}{1} \times \square = \square$

5. $36 \div 9 = \square \times \square = \square$

6. $24 \div 3 = \square \times \square = \square$

7. $44 \div 4 = \square \times \square = \square$

8. $56 \div 7 = \square \times \square = \square$

9. $64 \div 8 = \square \times \square = \square$

10. $75 \div 3 = \square \times \square = \square$

How to Divide Fractions

Division of fractions is identical to the reciprocal multiplying you just practiced with whole numbers. To divide one fraction by another, multiply by the reciprocal of the divisor. Note that when fractional divisions are written in standard form, the divisor is always the second number. You always multiply by the reciprocal of the second number.

When you divide fractions, always multiply by the reciprocal of the divisor, which is the second fraction. Never "flip" the first fraction and never "flip" both fractions.

Look at the examples below.

Example 1

$$\frac{3}{4} \div \frac{2}{3}$$

$$\downarrow$$

$$\frac{3}{4} \times \frac{3}{2}$$

$$\downarrow$$

$$\frac{3}{4} \times \frac{3}{2} = \frac{9}{8} = 1\frac{1}{8}$$

Example 2

$$\frac{3}{16} \div \frac{1}{2}$$

$$\downarrow$$

$$\frac{3}{16} \times \frac{2}{1}$$

$$\downarrow$$

$$\frac{3}{\overset{}{\underset{8}{\cancel{16}}}} \times \frac{\overset{1}{\cancel{2}}}{1} = \frac{3}{8}$$

In example 2, you can divide by common factors after you rewrite the division as a multiplication problem. However, you can't divide by common factors across a division sign. Note that in the first line of example 1, the 3s can't be divided.

When you have a division of fractions problem, there is no dividing by common factors until you have found the reciprocal and are *multiplying*. You can only divide by common factors in multiplication problems!

Quick Quiz E

Directions: Divide the following and express your answers in simplest form.

1. $\dfrac{2}{3} \div \dfrac{1}{4} =$ _____

2. $\dfrac{5}{8} \div \dfrac{3}{12} =$ _____

3. $\dfrac{2}{7} \div \dfrac{3}{14} =$ _____

4. $\dfrac{5}{9} \div \dfrac{1}{3} =$ _____

5. $\dfrac{4}{7} \div \dfrac{6}{14} =$ _____

6. $\dfrac{3}{8} \div \dfrac{3}{4} =$ _____

7. $\dfrac{5}{12} \div \dfrac{10}{18} =$ _____

8. $\dfrac{8}{19} \div \dfrac{4}{38} =$ _____

9. $\dfrac{2}{3} \div \dfrac{3}{4} =$ _____

10. $\dfrac{5}{9} \div \dfrac{6}{7} =$ _____

Multiplication and Division with Mixed Numbers

Rewriting Mixed Numbers as Fractions

Unlike adding and subtracting, you don't multiply and divide mixed numbers by working first with the fractions and then the whole numbers. Instead, you must rewrite both mixed numbers as fractions. Then, you multiply or divide the fractions in the same way as you did earlier in the chapter.

To rewrite a mixed number as a fraction, follow the formula below to get the numerator of the fraction:

$$\frac{(\text{Whole Number} \times \text{Denominator}) + \text{Numerator}}{\text{Original Denominator}}$$

The denominator stays the same from the mixed number to the fraction because the size of the parts has not changed. Watch how to rewrite $3\dfrac{5}{8}$ as a fraction, following the formula above:

1. $3 \times 8 = 24$ (Whole number × denominator)

2. $24 + 5 = 29$ (Add the numerator to the product.)

3. $3\dfrac{5}{8} = \dfrac{29}{8}$ (Put the sum over the denominator.)

To recap: First, the denominator (8) is multiplied by the whole number (3). Then, the numerator (5) is added to the product (24). That makes the new numerator (29). The denominator for the new fraction is the same as the old denominator (8).

Here's another example: Rewrite $2\dfrac{1}{3}$ as a fraction:

1. $2 \times 3 = 6$ (Whole number × denominator)
2. $6 + 1 = 7$ (Add the numerator to the product.)
3. $2\dfrac{1}{3} = \dfrac{7}{3}$ (Put the sum over the denominator.)

Quick Quiz F

Directions: Express the mixed numbers below as fractions. Refer to the examples above if you need a map to follow.

1. $9\dfrac{2}{7} =$ _____

2. $8\dfrac{3}{4} =$ _____

3. $2\dfrac{1}{2} =$ _____

4. $3\dfrac{1}{5} =$ _____

5. $5\dfrac{1}{4} =$ _____

6. $4\dfrac{2}{3} =$ _____

7. $6\dfrac{3}{4} =$ _____

8. $7\dfrac{3}{5} =$ _____

9. $5\dfrac{6}{7} =$ _____

10. $6\dfrac{7}{8} =$ _____

How to Multiply and Divide Mixed Numbers

When you multiply or divide mixed numbers, first rewrite any mixed numbers as fractions. If the problem is a multiplication problem, look for common factors that you can divide. Then, multiply. You can give your answer as a fraction or rewrite it as a mixed number. If the problem is a division problem, rewrite it as multiplication by finding the reciprocal of the second fraction. Continue as if the problem started out as multiplication.

> You'll often have great numbers in the numerators of the fractions, so it's very important to look for common factors and divide by them before you multiply.

Quick Quiz G

Directions: Change to fractions, then multiply or divide as indicated.

1. $3\frac{1}{2} \times 2\frac{1}{2} =$ ___

2. $2\frac{3}{4} \times 3\frac{1}{2} =$ ___

3. $5\frac{1}{3} \div 1\frac{1}{2} =$ ___

4. $3\frac{2}{3} \div 2\frac{1}{4} =$ __

5. $4\frac{3}{8} \times 3\frac{5}{6} =$ ___

6. $4\frac{7}{12} \div 2\frac{2}{6} =$ __

7. $4\frac{2}{7} \times 3\frac{7}{21} =$ ___

8. $3\frac{5}{7} \div 2\frac{8}{21} =$ __

9. $4\frac{3}{8} \div 3\frac{7}{12} =$ __

10. $2\frac{3}{7} \times 5\frac{3}{8} =$ ___

Answers to Quick Quizzes

Answers to Quick Quiz A

1. $\dfrac{1}{2}$

2. $\dfrac{1}{8}$

3. $\dfrac{4}{21}$

4. $\dfrac{5}{14}$

5. $\dfrac{1}{4}$

6. $\dfrac{3}{10}$

7. $\dfrac{3}{4}$

8. $\dfrac{1}{3}$

Answers to Quick Quiz B

1. $\dfrac{1}{3}$

2. $\dfrac{1}{4}$

3. $\dfrac{2}{9}$

4. $\dfrac{3}{34}$

5. $\dfrac{5}{24}$

6. $\dfrac{3}{22}$

7. $\dfrac{1}{4}$

8. $\dfrac{3}{8}$

9. 1

10. $\dfrac{1}{3}$

Answers to Quick Quiz C

1. $\dfrac{1}{5}$

2. $\dfrac{1}{8}$

3. $\dfrac{1}{27}$

4. 9

5. 27

6. 345

7. $\dfrac{3}{2}$

8. $\dfrac{83}{8}$

9. $\dfrac{69}{17}$

10. $\dfrac{517}{123}$

Answers to Quick Quiz D

1. $\frac{1}{3}$, 6

2. $\frac{1}{5}$, 7

3. $\frac{1}{5}$, 3

4. $\frac{1}{4}$, 4

5. $\frac{36}{1}$, $\frac{1}{9}$, 4

6. $\frac{24}{1}$, $\frac{1}{3}$, 8

7. $\frac{44}{1}$, $\frac{1}{4}$, 11

8. $\frac{56}{1}$, $\frac{1}{7}$, 8

9. $\frac{64}{1}$, $\frac{1}{8}$, 8

10. $\frac{75}{1}$, $\frac{1}{3}$, 25

Answers to Quick Quiz E

1. $\frac{8}{3}$ or $2\frac{2}{3}$

2. $\frac{5}{2}$ or $2\frac{1}{2}$

3. $\frac{4}{3}$ or $1\frac{1}{3}$

4. $\frac{5}{3}$ or $1\frac{2}{3}$

5. $\frac{4}{3}$ or $1\frac{1}{3}$

6. $\frac{1}{2}$

7. $\frac{3}{4}$

8. 4

9. $\frac{8}{9}$

10. $\frac{35}{54}$

Answers to Quick Quiz F

1. $\frac{65}{7}$

2. $\frac{35}{4}$

3. $\frac{5}{2}$

4. $\frac{16}{5}$

5. $\frac{21}{4}$

6. $\frac{14}{3}$

7. $\frac{27}{4}$

8. $\frac{38}{5}$

9. $\frac{41}{7}$

10. $\frac{55}{8}$

Answers to Quick Quiz G

1. $8\dfrac{3}{4}$

2. $9\dfrac{5}{8}$

3. $3\dfrac{5}{9}$

4. $1\dfrac{17}{27}$

5. $16\dfrac{37}{48}$

6. $1\dfrac{27}{28}$

7. $14\dfrac{2}{7}$

8. $1\dfrac{14}{25}$

9. $1\dfrac{19}{86}$

10. $13\dfrac{3}{56}$

Place Value 10
and Decimals

Place-Value Numeration

The *decimal system* is used to represent numbers. The decimal system of writing numerals is based on groupings of tens. It has several important features, which we'll examine in this chapter.

Digits

A single number, such as 1, 2, or 3, is called a digit. There are ten digits: 0, 1, 2, 3, 4, 5, 6, 7, 8, 9. Using any combination of these ten digits, you can represent any number, no matter how small or great that number's value.

Places

In the decimal system, the place the digit holds within the number is important. Take a look at numbers *A, B, C,* and *D* in the chart below.

	Th	H	T	U
A				3
B		3		
C			3	
D	3			

In the chart, *A, B, C,* and *D* are each represented by a single digit—3, but they *represent* four different numbers. When those numbers are removed from the columns that they are in, zeros would have to be added to *B, C,* and *D* to show the place where the digit 3 actually belongs. They would be written:

$$
\begin{aligned}
A &= 3 \\
B &= 300 \\
C &= 30 \\
D &= 3{,}000
\end{aligned}
$$

There is a big difference between three and three thousand, but if you didn't consider the place in which each digit is written, they would seem to be the same.

Remember, the decimal system is based on the number ten. This tells you the relationship of one place to another within any decimal numeral. Look at the table below.

...	10×100	10×10	10×1	1	...
A				3	
B		3			
C			3		
D	3				

Notice that in the table, the column with a number furthest to the right has number 1 as its heading. To find its true value, any digit written in that column must be multiplied by one. Here, there's a three in that column:

$$3 \times 1 = 3$$

So A is worth 3.

Now, move left one column. You'll see that the next place is worth ten times as much as the column to its right. Since $10 \times 1 = 10$, any digit written in that place is worth 10 times its face value. So, for C, the value is:

$$3 \times 10, \text{ which is } 30.$$

Move left again. The third column from the right is worth ten times as much as the place to its right:

$$10 \times 10 = 100$$

So B, which is written in that place, actually is worth 3 times 100. D is 10 times greater than B. The three dots to the left of the thousands place are there to indicate that as you continue to move to the left one place at a time, each place will be worth ten times as much as the place to its right. The three dots on the far right indicate that the decimal system and the pattern of tens continue for numbers smaller than one. You will learn more about this later in this chapter.

Zero as a Placeholder

Numbers aren't usually written in tables that look like the one you just saw. So we need to have some way of showing what place a digit is in, even though it isn't written in a column. That's where the idea of a *placeholder* comes in. A placeholder is a digit that doesn't have any value of its own, but will fill up the holes left in a number when that number is written without column headings. Zero does just that. If you look back at B, you'll notice that there are two empty places to the right of the digit 3. When we write *B* without the columns, we use zeros to fill in, or hold the place of, those empty columns. So *B* is written as 300, with the two empty places filled by placeholder zeroes.

Quick Quiz A

Directions: Look at the following table. Write the number in place-value form (with the appropriate placeholders).

	1,000,000	100,000	10,000	1,000	100	10	1	
A						6		A _____
B				5				B _____
C			8					C _____
D		7						D _____
E					4			E _____
F			5		6			F _____
G	2		8			3		G _____
H		9		6			2	H _____
I	3			9				I _____

Decimals

What Is a Decimal?

Decimals are important because they show you how to use the decimal system (the way you express all whole numbers) for numbers less than one. Decimals follow all the rules of place-value numbers and easily fit in with whole number operations.

The word decimal means **tenth**. When you move from left to right across a place-value chart, each place is worth one tenth as much as the one to its immediate left:

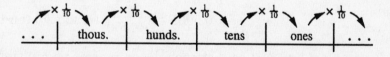

Notice that in the chart above that there's no beginning and no end. As you move along the chart from left to right, each place is multiplied by one tenth to find the value of the place to the right. After the ones place comes the decimal point. That **decimal point** is used to separate the whole numbers from the fractions. Consider the value of each 3 in the place-value chart below.

Write	...100's	10's	1's	10ths	100ths	1000ths...	Value
300	3						300
30		3					30
3			3				3
.3				3			$\frac{3}{10}$
.03					3		$\frac{3}{100}$
.003						3	$\frac{3}{1000}$

All digits to the left of the decimal point are whole numbers. All digits to the right of the decimal point are fractional numbers.

Examine the following examples, and then try the exercises that follow.

Example 1

$$0.5 = \frac{5}{10} \text{ (read as 5 tenths)}$$

Example 2

$$0.05 = \frac{5}{100} \text{ (read as 5 hundredths)}$$

Example 3

$$0.005 = \frac{5}{1,000} \text{ (read as 5 thousandths)}$$

Example 4

$$0.0005 = \frac{5}{10,000} \text{ (read as 5 ten-thousandths)}$$

- Notice that each denominator is a multiple of ten.
- Note that the number of zeroes in the denominator is the same as the number of places there are to the right of the decimal point.

Quick Quiz B

Directions: Write the fraction or mixed number that is equivalent to the decimals.

1. 0.3 = ___

2. 0.7 = ___

3. 0.04 = ___

4. 0.06 = ___

5. 0.005 = ___

6. 0.003 = ___

7. 0.0002 = ___

8. 0.0006 = ___

Directions: Write the decimal that is equivalent to the fractions. Don't forget to put placeholder zeros between the decimal point and the number if you need them.

9. $\dfrac{7}{10}$ = ___

10. $\dfrac{9}{10}$ = ___

11. $\dfrac{5}{100}$ = ___

12. $\dfrac{1}{1,000}$ = ___

13. $\dfrac{15}{100}$ = ___

14. $\dfrac{6}{1,000}$ = ___

15. $\dfrac{5}{10}$ = ___

16. $\dfrac{4}{100,000}$ = ___

When a decimal has more than a single digit, it is named by the place value of the digit farthest to the right. For example, 0.17 would be read as 17 hundredths because the 7 is in the hundredths place. The number 0.23 is 23 hundredths, since the 3 is in the hundredths place, and 0.024 is 24 thousandths since the 4 is in the thousandths place. Also, 0.345 is read as three hundred forty-five thousandths, and 0.0216 is two hundred sixteen ten-thousandths. Notice that there are never any commas used to the right of the decimal point to help you read the number.

When you read a whole number with a decimal, you write or say the word "and" when you get to the decimal point. For example, the number 4.25 is read as 4 *and* 25 hundredths.

Quick Quiz C

Directions: Name these decimals.

1. 0.24 _____

2. 0.68 _____

3. 0.069 _____

4. 0.053 _____

5. 0.437 _____

6. 0.619 _____

7. 0.0085 _____

8. 0.0136 _____

9. 0.0148 _____

10. 7.045 _____

Rewriting Common Fractions as Decimals

Certain common fractions are easily expressed as decimals. That's true of fractions whose denominators are multiples of ten, such as tenths, hundredths, and thousandths. Other common fractions can be rewritten as decimals by first writing equivalent fractions with denominators that are multiples of ten. Look at the examples below.

Example 1

$$\frac{1}{4} = \frac{}{100} \rightarrow \frac{1}{4} = \frac{25}{100} = 0.25$$

4 does not divide 10 perfectly, but it divides 100 evenly, 25 times.

Example 2

$$\frac{3}{5} = \frac{}{10} \rightarrow \frac{3}{5} = \frac{6}{10} = 0.6$$

5 divides 10 perfectly, so make 10 the denominator of your equivalent fraction.

Example 3

$$\frac{3}{8} = \frac{}{1000} \rightarrow \frac{3}{8} = \frac{375}{1000} = .375$$

8 divides neither 10 nor 100 perfectly. It does divide 1000 evenly, 125 times.

Quick Quiz D

Directions: Express the following common fractions as decimal fractions.

1. $\frac{3}{4} = \frac{}{100} = $ _____

2. $\frac{1}{2} = \frac{}{10} = $ _____

3. $\frac{2}{5} = \frac{}{10} = $ _____

4. $\frac{5}{8} = \frac{}{1,000} = $ _____

5. $\frac{7}{20} = \frac{}{100} = $ _____

6. $\frac{7}{8} = \frac{}{1,000} = $ _____

7. $\frac{9}{50} = \frac{}{100} = $ _____

8. $\frac{11}{25} = \frac{}{100} = $ _____

9. $\frac{13}{50} = \frac{}{100} = $ _____

10. $\frac{13}{20} = \frac{}{100} = $ _____

You probably use some common fractions and decimals in your everyday life. You should memorize them so you never have to spend time figuring them out. They include: $\frac{1}{2} = 0.5,$ $\frac{1}{4} = 0.25,$ $\frac{3}{4} = 0.75,$ $\frac{1}{5} = 0.2,$ $\frac{1}{10} = 0.1$

Unfortunately, not all fractions will rewrite as easily as equivalent fractions with denominators that are multiples of ten. However, there's a way to rewrite any common fraction as a decimal. That method is to divide the numerator of any fraction by its denominator. Check out the following examples.

Example 1

$$\frac{1}{4} \rightarrow 4\overline{)1} \rightarrow 4\overline{)1.00} \rightarrow 4\overline{)1.00}^{.25}$$

To find the decimal equivalent of $\frac{1}{4}$, 1 must be divided by 4. Since 4 doesn't' divide 1 a whole number of times, you modify the dividend. To do that, place the decimal point after the 1, and add two zeroes (1.00 = 1). Place a decimal point in the quotient over the decimal point in the dividend and get the decimal 0.25.

Example 2

$$\frac{3}{5} \rightarrow 5\overline{)3} \rightarrow 5\overline{)3.0} \rightarrow 5\overset{.6}{\overline{)3.0}}$$

To divide 3 by 5, one zero after the decimal point is enough, even though adding a second zero after the decimal point won't hurt the answer (since 0.60 = 0.6). Continue as in example 1.

Example 3

$$\frac{1}{3} \rightarrow 3\overline{)1} \rightarrow 3\overline{)1.00} \rightarrow 3\overset{.3\overline{3}}{\overline{)1.00}}$$

No matter how many zeroes are added after the decimal point, 3s will keep appearing in the quotient. The fraction $\frac{1}{3}$ translates to what's known as a repeating decimal. The bar over the second 3 in the quotient 3 indicates that the 3 keeps repeating. The bar should be written over all the digits that repeat. For example, $\frac{9}{11} = 0.\overline{81}$, which is 0.8181818181...

> To rewrite any fraction as a decimal, divide the numerator by the denominator. Use the bar notation to indicate repeating decimals.

Rounding Decimals

It's often unnecessary to express a quantity with the exact number. For example, when estimating the crowd at a baseball game, the fact that 48,143 persons attended is usually an overly accurate piece of information. It's often enough to say that there were about 48,000 people there. 48,000 is the crowd size rounded to the nearest thousand.

To round a number, you need to look at two things. First, you need to look at the place to which the number is to be rounded. Second, you have to look at the digit in the place just to the right of the place that you plan to round the number. Review the examples on the following page.

Example 1
Round 34,567 to the nearest hundred.

3 4, <u>5</u> 6 7 ⇒   3 4, <u>5</u>   <u>6</u> 7 ⇒ 3 4, <u>6</u> 0 0
     ↑   ↑   ↑

Place to be rounded to.   5 or greater.   Rounded up to 6.

Example 2
Round 34,567 to the nearest 10,000.

<u>3</u> 4, 5 6 7 ⇒   <u>3</u> <u>4</u>, 5 6 7 ⇒   <u>3</u> 0, 0 0 0
↑   ↑   ↑

Place to be rounded to.   Less than 5.   Stays a 3.

Example 3
Round 27.635 to the nearest tenth.

2 7. <u>6</u> 3 5 ⇒   2 7. <u>6</u> <u>3</u> 5 ⇒ 2 7. <u>6</u>
       ↑   ↑   ↑

Place to be rounded to. Less than 5.   Stays a 6. Drop other places.

Example 4
Round 27.635 to the nearest hundredth.

2 7. 6 <u>3</u> 5 ⇒   2 7. 6 <u>3</u> <u>5</u> ⇒ 2 7. 6 4
          ↑   ↑   ↑

                                                    Rounded up to 4.
Place to be rounded to. 5 or greater.   Drop other places.

When you round a number, the only digit that controls the rounding is the digit to the right of the rounding place. The digits that are in the number later don't affect the rounding. So if you are asked to round 65,199 to the nearest thousand, your answer will be 65,000. Those nines don't make any difference.

When you round a whole number, the place rounded to is the last one in which a non-zero digit appears. Each place to the right contains a zero (see how 34,567 to the nearest 10,000 became 30,000). When you round a decimal, however, the place to which you round is the last digit that will appear in the rounded number. No zeroes are inserted to follow it; you just drop those places (see examples 3 and 4).

Quick Quiz E

Directions: Complete the following exercises. If you need to, use the examples above as your guide.

Round to the nearest

	hundred	ten	tenth	hundredth
1. 4562.738	_____	_____	_____	_____
2. 328.4929	_____	_____	_____	_____
3. 255.555	_____	_____	_____	_____
4. 8134.8134	_____	_____	_____	_____
5. 2121.9192	_____	_____	_____	_____

Since many fractions don't rewrite perfectly as decimals, you often have to round them. You already saw that $\frac{1}{3}$ translates to $0.333\overline{333}$ when it is written as a decimal. Many fractions rewrite as repeating decimals. It's good practice to round decimals to the nearest hundredth if the decimal repeats or does not end. To be able to round to the nearest hundredth, you need to work a decimal out to the thousandths place. The digit in the thousandths place will tell you whether to leave the digit in the hundredths place as it is or to round it up to the next greater digit. Keep this in mind as you try the following exercises.

Quick Quiz F

Directions: Express each common fraction as a decimal. When there are more than 2 decimal places, round to the nearest hundredth.

1. $\frac{5}{16} =$ _____   **6.** $\frac{7}{12} =$ _____

2. $\frac{5}{9} =$ _____   **7.** $\frac{4}{7} =$ _____

3. $\frac{2}{3} =$ _____   **8.** $\frac{5}{8} =$ _____

4. $\frac{4}{5} =$ _____   **9.** $\frac{11}{20} =$ _____

5. $\frac{8}{11} =$ _____   **10.** $\frac{17}{35} =$ _____

Answers to Quick Quizzes

Answers to Quick Quiz A

1. A   60

2. B   5,000

3. C   80,000

4. D   700,000

5. E   400

6. F   50,600

7. G   2,080,030

8. H   906,002

9. I   3,000,090

Answers to Quick Quiz B

1. $\dfrac{3}{10}$

2. $\dfrac{7}{10}$

3. $\dfrac{4}{100}$

4. $\dfrac{6}{100}$

5. $\dfrac{5}{1,000}$

6. $\dfrac{3}{1,000}$

7. $\dfrac{2}{10,000}$

8. $\dfrac{6}{10,000}$

9. 0.7

10. 0.9

11. 0.05

12. 0.001

13. 0.15

14. 0.006

15. 0.5

16. 0.00004

Answers to Quick Quiz C

1. 24 hundredths

2. 68 hundredths

3. 69 thousandths

4. 53 thousandths

5. 437 thousandths

6. 619 thousandths

7. 85 ten-thousandths

8. 136 ten-thousandths

9. 148 hundred-thousandths

10. 7 and 45 thousandths

Answers to Quick Quiz D

1. 0.75
2. 0.5
3. 0.4
4. 0.625
5. 0.35
6. 0.875
7. 0.18
8. 0.44
9. 0.26
10. 0.65

Answers to Quick Quiz E

1. 4600, 4560, 4562.7, 4562.74
2. 300, 330, 328.5, 328.49
3. 300, 260, 255.6, 255.56
4. 8100, 8130, 8134.8, 8134.81
5. 2100, 2120, 2121.9, 2121.92

Answers to Quick Quiz F

1. 0.31
2. 0.56
3. 0.67
4. 0.80
5. 0.73
6. 0.58
7. 0.57
8. 0.63
9. 0.55
10. 0.49

Operations with Decimals 11

Adding Decimals

There's only one key to the addition of decimals: **The decimal points must be lined up one under the other.** The decimal point in the sum needs to be beneath the decimal points in the addition problem, then the numbers are added. If a number doesn't have a decimal point, then it's a whole number. Whole numbers have an "invisible decimal point" to the right of the ones place. You can put the decimal point there when you line up the numbers for the problem. To see how this works, take a look at the examples below.

Example 1

$$2.4 + 1.8 + 3.72$$

$$
\begin{array}{r}
2.4 \\
1.8 \\
+\ 3.72 \\
\hline
\end{array}
\qquad
\begin{array}{r}
2.4 \\
1.8 \\
+\ 3.72 \\
\hline
7.92
\end{array}
$$

First align the decimal points.   Then add.

Example 2

$$3.6 + 0.074 + 59 + 16.08$$

$$
\begin{array}{r}
3.6 \\
0.074 \\
59. \\
+\ 16.08 \\
\hline
\end{array}
\qquad
\begin{array}{r}
3.6 \\
0.074 \\
59. \\
+\ 16.08 \\
\hline
78.754
\end{array}
$$

The decimal points must be lined up in a column, one right beneath the other, when you add and subtract decimals. Keeping the decimals lined up keeps your place-value columns lined up, too.

Quick Quiz A

Directions: Solve the addition problems below.

1.
$$\begin{array}{r} 3.4 \\ 2.86 \\ +\ 12.5 \\ \hline \end{array}$$

2.
$$\begin{array}{r} 5.61 \\ 0.007 \\ +\ 21.0 \\ \hline \end{array}$$

3.
$$\begin{array}{r} 6.81 \\ 0.009 \\ 5.73 \\ +\ 24.0 \\ \hline \end{array}$$

4. 17.2 + 8.09 + 4.6

5. 61.9 + 3.85 + 596 + 0.35

6. 63 + 0.34 + 5.21 + 0.098 + 351.7 + 84.2

Subtracting Decimals

Subtraction of decimals is done the same way as addition of decimals: by lining the decimal points up one beneath the other. There is one exception, though, and it is shown in the example below:

Example

$$8.6 - 3.425 =$$

The subtraction is first rewritten in column form, lining up the decimal points one below the other.

$$\begin{array}{r} 8.6 \\ -\ 3.425 \\ \hline \end{array}$$
Here, the 2 and the 5 have nothing to be subtracted from.

$$\begin{array}{r} 8.600 \\ -\ 3.425 \\ \hline \end{array}$$
Add placeholder zeroes to fill in the spaces above the 2 and the 5. Remember, the values of 8.6 and 8.600 are identical.

$$\begin{array}{r} \overset{5}{8}.\overset{9}{\cancel{6}}\ \overset{10}{\cancel{0}}\ 0 \\ -\ 3.\ 4\ 2\ 5 \\ \hline 5.\ 1\ 7\ 5 \end{array}$$
Now you can subtract. You'll have to do some renaming. Note where the decimal point is in the difference.

Putting zeroes after the last significant digit to the right of the decimal point doesn't change the number's value. For example: 0.3 = 0.30 = 0.300

Quick Quiz B

Directions: Now it's time to try subtracting some decimals on your own.

1.
$$\begin{array}{r} 8.69 \\ -3.54 \\ \hline \end{array}$$

2.
$$\begin{array}{r} 15.7 \\ -5.9 \\ \hline \end{array}$$

3.
$$\begin{array}{r} 36.4 \\ -7.8 \\ \hline \end{array}$$

4. 125 – 0.02

5. 67.1 – 0.875

6. 143.5 – 68.9

Multiplying Decimals

Multiplying decimals works the same as multiplying whole numbers. However, there's a trick to where the decimal point is placed in the answer. You'll probably be able to figure out the trick by examining the table below. Look for the pattern of the placement of the decimal point. Each line contains a single multiplication, first expressed in common fractions and then in decimals.

Multiply	Product	Multiply	Product
$\frac{1}{10} \times \frac{1}{10}$	$\frac{1}{100}$	0.1 × 0.1	0.01
$\frac{1}{10} \times \frac{1}{100}$	$\frac{1}{1,000}$	0.1 × 0.01	0.001
$\frac{1}{100} \times \frac{1}{100}$	$\frac{1}{10,000}$	0.01 × 0.01	0.0001
$\frac{1}{10} \times \frac{1}{1,000}$	$\frac{1}{10,000}$	0.1 × 0.001	0.0001
$\frac{1}{100} \times \frac{1}{1,000}$	$\frac{1}{100,000}$	0.01 × 0.001	0.00001
$\frac{1}{1,000} \times \frac{1}{1,000}$	$\frac{1}{1,000,000}$	0.001 × 0.001	0.000001
$\frac{1}{10} \times \frac{1}{10,000}$	$\frac{1}{100,000}$	0.1 × 0.0001	0.00001

Count up the number of digits to the right of the decimal point in each of the multiplications above. Then count up the number of digits to the right of the decimal point in each product. Do you see the pattern? Here it is:

> When multiplying decimals, the number of digits to the right of the decimal point in the product will equal the total number of digits to the right of the points in the two numbers being multiplied.

To see how counting digits to the right of the decimal point works in other problems, look at the examples below. You don't need to pay attention to the decimal points while multiplying since the decimal point is placed after the product is found.

Example 1

$$
\begin{array}{r}
2.5 \leftarrow 1 \text{ digit to the right} \\
\times 1.2 \leftarrow 1 \text{ digit to the right} \\
\hline
50 \qquad\qquad 2 \text{ digits to the right in all.} \\
250 \\
\hline
300 \rightarrow \qquad \rightarrow \quad 3.\underbrace{00}
\end{array}
$$

Two digits to the right.

Example 2

$$
\begin{array}{r}
7.9 \quad \leftarrow \qquad 1 \text{ digit to the right} \\
\times .002 \quad \leftarrow \qquad 3 \text{ digits to the right} \\
\hline
158 \qquad\quad 4 \text{ digits to the right in all.}
\end{array}
$$

$$.\underbrace{0158}$$

4 digits to the right.

Example 3

$$
\begin{array}{r}
.006 \\
\times .002
\end{array} \Big\} \leftarrow 6 \text{ digits to the right in all.}
$$

$$12 \rightarrow \qquad \rightarrow \quad 0.\underbrace{000012}$$

Six digits to the right.

Quick Quiz C

Directions: Place the decimal point in the correct place in each product.

1.	$\begin{array}{r} 12.4 \\ \times\,.01 \\ \hline 124 \end{array}$	**4.**	$\begin{array}{r} 7.55 \\ \times\,.13 \\ \hline 9815 \end{array}$
2.	$\begin{array}{r} 3.56 \\ \times\,.12 \\ \hline 4272 \end{array}$	**5.**	$\begin{array}{r} .214 \\ \times\,.001 \\ \hline 214 \end{array}$
3.	$\begin{array}{r} 4.7 \\ \times\,1.6 \\ \hline 752 \end{array}$	**6.**	$\begin{array}{r} .715 \\ \times\,.008 \\ \hline 5720 \end{array}$

> To multiply decimals, first multiply the same way you do with whole numbers. Then after you have multiplied (and added if necessary), place the decimal point.

Now that you have practiced placing the decimal point, try doing the whole problem. You can estimate to make sure your answers make sense. For example, 21.5×4.2 is about 21×4, which is 84. So when you place the decimal point, be sure you get something close to 84, not 0.84 or 8.4!

Quick Quiz D

Directions: Multiply the following and then place the decimal point correctly.

1.	$\begin{array}{r} 5.8 \\ \times.7 \\ \hline \end{array}$	**4.**	$\begin{array}{r} .96 \\ \times 2.7 \\ \hline \end{array}$
2.	$\begin{array}{r} .35 \\ \times 2 \\ \hline \end{array}$	**5.**	$\begin{array}{r} .085 \\ \times.31 \\ \hline \end{array}$
3.	$\begin{array}{r} .63 \\ \times.6 \\ \hline \end{array}$	**6.**	$\begin{array}{r} .058 \\ \times.012 \\ \hline \end{array}$

Multiplying and Dividing by Powers of Ten

Multiplying and dividing by powers of ten relies on patterns. Any whole number can be multiplied by 10 simply by adding a zero onto the end of the number. For example:

$$10 \times 2 \text{ is } 20, 10 \times 8 = 80, 10 \times 35 = 350, \text{ and } 10 \times 237 = 2{,}370.$$

To multiply a whole number by 100, attach two zeroes:

$$3 \times 100 = 300; 46 \times 100 = 4{,}600; 342 \times 100 = 34{,}200$$

To multiply a whole number by 1,000, attach three zeroes:

$$6 \times 1{,}000 = 6{,}000; 57 \times 1{,}000 = 57{,}000; 416 \times 1{,}000 = 416{,}000$$

To multiply by 10,000, attach four zeroes; to multiply by 100,000 attach five zeroes, and so on.

This method is an easy way to deal with multiplying whole numbers by powers of ten. Now that you are familiar with the meaning of a decimal point in a number, here's another explanation for multiplying by powers of ten:

- To multiply by 10, move the decimal point 1 place to the right.
- To multiply by 100, move the decimal point 2 places to the right.
- To multiply by 1,000, move the decimal point 3 places to the right.

To multiply a number by any power of ten, move the decimal point the same number of places to the right as there are zeroes in the power of ten that you are multiplying by.

If the decimal place moves past the last digit of the number, fill the empty places in with zeroes. For example:

$$4.5 \times 1{,}000 = 45\_\_. = 4{,}500.$$

This explanation is the actual process that occurs when zeroes are attached. It also applies to numbers containing decimal fractions. Study the table below.

Number	×10	×100	×1,000	×10,000	×100,000
23	230	2,300	23,000	230,000	2,300,000
3.4	34	340	3,400	34,000	340,000
.59	5.9	59	590	5,900	59,000
.028	.28	2.8	28	280	2,800
.0046	.046	.46	4.6	46	460
.00081	.0081	.081	.81	8.1	81

This way of multiplying by powers of 10 also helps explain how to divide by powers of 10. Since division is the "undoing" of multiplication, it makes sense that when dividing by powers of ten, you do the opposite of what you do when multiplying. This means that the decimal point must be moved to the left the same number of places as there are zeroes in the multiple of ten that you are dividing by. As with multiplication, if the decimal moves to the left of the first digit of the number, fill in empty places with placeholder zeroes. Take a look at the following table.

Number	÷10	÷100	÷1,000	÷10,000	÷100,000
23	2.3	.23	.023	.0023	.00023
3.4	.34	.034	.0034	.00034	.000034
567	56.7	5.67	.567	.0567	.00567
8,936	893.6	89.36	8.936	.8936	.08936
45,382	4,538.2	453.82	45.382	4.5382	.45382
732,971	73,297.1	7,329.71	732.971	73.2971	7.32971

Quick Quiz E

Directions: Multiply each number below by the stated multiplier.

1. 10 x 3.4 =

2. 10 x 0.62 =

3. 10 x 41.7 =

4. 100 x 5.9 =

5. 100 x 0.82 =

6. 100 x 63.4 =

7. 1,000 x 9.3 =

8. 1,000 x 0.93 =

9. 1,000 x 82.7 =

10. 1,000 x 0.095 =

Directions: Divide each number by the stated divisor.

11. 3.4 ÷ 10 =

12. 0.62 ÷ 10 =

13. 41.7 ÷ 10 =

14. 5.9 ÷ 100 =

15. 0.82 ÷ 100 =

16. 63.4 ÷ 100 =

17. 9.3 ÷ 1,000 =

18. 0.93 ÷ 1,000 =

19. 82.7 ÷ 1,000 =

20. 0.095 ÷ 1,000 =

The ability to quickly multiply and divide by powers of ten by moving the decimal point to the right or the left is a useful skill. You can learn it with a little practice and it will save you a lot of time in your work. If you think that you need more practice, make up lists of numbers with their decimal points in various places, and then practice multiplying and dividing by moving the decimal point. You can check your work on a calculator. Understanding this skill will help you understand the division of decimal.

Dividing Decimals

When two numbers are to be divided, multiplying both of those numbers by the same amount does not affect the quotient. Read that last sentence over again, to be certain that you understand what it means. Then look at the illustration of that statement below:

$$3\overline{)15}^{\,5} \quad \rightarrow \times 100 \rightarrow \quad 300\overline{)1500}^{\,5}$$

$$\downarrow$$
$$\times 10$$
$$\downarrow$$

$$30\overline{)150}^{\,5}$$

Across, both divisor and dividend are multiplied by 100. Down, both divisor and dividend are multiplied by 10. All three problems have a quotient of 5.

The first thing you need to know in order to divide decimals is that you never actually divide by a decimal. It may sound odd, but it's true. In order to divide by a decimal, you need to first change that decimal to a whole number. Carefully study the examples below, and you'll see that the process is easier to do than it is to describe.

Example 1

$.6.\overline{)1.8}$ To change .6 to a whole number, the decimal point must be moved to the right one place.

$6.\overline{)1.8.}$ Moving that decimal point is the same as multiplying by 10. In order to avoid changing the problem, the decimal in the dividend must also be multiplied by 10.

$6\overline{)18.}^{\,\cdot}$ The decimal point in the quotient is then placed right above the decimal point in the dividend.

$6\overline{)18}^{\,3}$ Dividing, you get a quotient of 3.

Example 2

$.09\overline{)\,.081}$ To change .09 to a whole number, multiply by 100. (That means moving the decimal point 2 places to the right.)

$.09.\overline{)\,08.1}$ Of course, if one decimal point is moved 2 places, so must the other one be moved.

$09.\overline{)\,08.1} = 9\overline{)\,8.1}$ The zeroes to the left of the first figures do not have any meaning, so drop them.

$9\overline{)\,8.1}$ Place the decimal point in the quotient right over the one in the dividend.

$9\overline{)\,8.1}^{\,.9}$ Divide, and get a quotient of 0.9

Example 3

$1.2\overline{)\,144}$ To change 1.2 to a whole number, move the decimal point one place to the right.

$1.2.\overline{)\,144.0}$ To move the decimal point in 144, attach a zero as a place-holder.

$12\overline{)\,1440.}$ Place the decimal point in the quotient above the decimal point in the dividend.

$12\overline{)\,1440}^{\,120}$ Divide and get a quotient of 120.

Notice that once the divisor has been made into a whole number by moving the decimal point and the dividend's decimal point has been moved and the point placed in the quotient, the actual division process is identical to division with integers. So, once you have reached this point, use the form of division you normally use to find the solution.

Example 4

$3.2\overline{)7.6}$ Most divisions do not come out evenly. This one begins as have all the others—by moving decimal points:

$3.\underline{2}\overline{)7.\underline{6}}$ Decimal points in the divisor and dividend are each moved one place.

$32\overline{)\overset{\cdot}{76.}}$ The decimal point in the quotient is then placed.

$$
\begin{array}{r}
2. \\
32\overline{)76.} \\
\underline{64} \\
12
\end{array}
$$

Dividing, you find that there are two 32s in 76. Remainders like R12 and fractional remainders like $\dfrac{12}{32}$ are not used when dividing decimals, so you have to keep dividing. Your remainder will be written as a decimal.

$$
\begin{array}{r}
2.3 \\
32\overline{)76.0} \\
\underline{64}\downarrow \\
12\,0 \\
\underline{96} \\
24
\end{array}
$$
Place a zero after the decimal point . . .

$$
\begin{array}{r}
2.37 \\
32\overline{)76.00} \\
\underline{64}\downarrow \\
120 \\
\underline{96}\downarrow \\
240 \\
\underline{224} \\
16
\end{array}
$$
. . . and, when needed, another zero . . .

$$
\begin{array}{r}
2.375 \\
32\overline{)76.000} \\
\underline{64}\downarrow \\
120 \\
\underline{96}\downarrow \\
240 \\
\underline{224}\downarrow \\
160 \\
\underline{160}
\end{array}
$$

... and, when needed, still another zero. If this zero had not yielded an exact ending, we would have rounded the answer back to the nearest hundredth.

Quick Quiz F

Directions: Divide the following and, where necessary, round the quotients to the nearest hundredth.

1. $0.2\overline{)6.70}$

2. $1.3\overline{).48}$

3. $2.5\overline{)64}$

4. $0.16\overline{)35.4}$

5. $.42\overline{)6.82}$

6. $4.7\overline{)0.685}$

Answers to Quick Quizzes

Answers to Quick Quiz A

1. 18.76

2. 26.617

3. 36.549

4. 29.89

5. 662.1

6. 504.548

Answers to Quick Quiz B

1. 5.15

2 9.8

3. 28.6

4. 124.98

5. 66.225

6. 74.6

Answers to Quick Quiz C

1. 0.124

2. 0.4272

3. 7.52

4. 0.9815

5. 0.000214

6. 0.005720

Answers to Quick Quiz D

1. 4.06

2. 0.7

3. 0.378

4. 2.592

5. 0.02635

6. 0.000696

Answers to Quick Quiz E

1. 34

2. 6.2

3. 417

4. 590

5. 82

6. 6,340

7. 9,300

8. 930

9. 82,700

10. 95

11. 0.34

12. 0.062

13. 4.17

14. 0.059

15. 0.0082

16. 0.634

17. 0.0093

18. 0.00093

19. 0.0827

20. 0.000095

Answers to Quick Quiz F

1. 33.5

2. 0.37

3. 25.6

4. 221.25

5. 16.24

6. 0.15

Introduction to Algebra

Algebra Basics 12

Constants and Variables in Algebra

Algebra is a type of math that helps solve word problems and helps to develop your abilities to analyze problems. Many people who don't know how algebra operations work are afraid of them. You shouldn't be. Algebra is a very useful tool. Two major parts of algebra, constants and variables, will help you understand what algebra is all about.

Constants

Any real number is a **constant**. 3 = 3 = 3. The value of a constant never changes. It's always the same. The number 25 means 25 now and will mean 25 later. It will always mean 25. It is a constant.

A constant may be a whole number, a fraction, a mixed number, or a decimal. It cannot, however, contain a letter. As soon as you see a letter in an expression, you know that it is a variable.

Quick Quiz A

Directions: Circle the answers that are constants.

1. 36

2. 251

3. y

4. $4n$

5. $\dfrac{4}{7}$

6. 0.0792

Variables

A **variable** is a symbol that takes the place of a number. Variables are usually written as a lower case letter, $a, b, c, \ldots x, y, z$. Sometimes, variables are written with capital letters, Greek letters, or even geometric symbols. Take a look at the following:

$$n = 4 + 7$$

In this math sentence, the variable n has been used to represent a number. You can find out what number n represents by combining the numbers on the right side of the equal sign. Since $7 + 4 = 11$, the following is true:

$$n = \mathbf{11}$$

Now, try this one:

$$n = 19 - 4$$

What number does n represent this time?

By subtracting the 4 from 19, you find that n represents 15. Notice that in two different math sentences, n has had two different values. The value of n has varied (or changed) from expression to expression. That makes n a variable.

Quick Quiz B

Directions: Mark the answers that are variables.

1. $3a$ **4.** 97

2. $\dfrac{m}{7}$ **5.** D

3. 19   **6.** Δ

The meaning of a variable (that is, the value it represents) can change from math sentence to math sentence. But within a single sentence, each time the same variable appears it must stand for the same number. Look at the following sentence.

$$n + 3 = 11 - n$$

If the first $n = 4$, then so must the second. If you substitute 4 for each n in that sentence, you get the following:

$$4 + 3 = 11 - 4$$
$$7 = 7$$

This is a true sentence. If, however, the second n had stood for anything but 4, the sentence would have been false.

Combining Variables

Since variables represent numbers, you can treat them like numbers. Variables can be added, subtracted, multiplied, and divided.

Adding

Any time you see the term *n*, it means that there's *one n* present. This seems obvious, but it's important to understanding how variables are combined. If there were 2 or more *n*s present, you would see them represented as 2*n*, 3*n*, 28*n*, etc. If there were no *n*s being represented (0*n*), you'd see no symbol at all. Zero *n*s is the same as plain 0. One *n* by itself therefore must mean 1*n*. However, the expression "1*n*" is rarely written. It's proper to simply write "*n*."

A number written next to a variable is called that variable's **coefficient**. In the expression 5*n*, *n*'s coefficient is 5. In the term 18*x*, *x*'s coefficient is 18. In the expression *r*, *r*'s coefficient is 1.

Quick Quiz C

Directions: Name the coefficient of each variable below.

1. 3*x*

2. 7*n*

3. *s*

4. 19*b*

5. *w*

6. $\frac{2}{3}h$

Remember, if you don't see a numerical coefficient next to a variable, that variable's coefficient is 1.

A **term** is a group of variables and their coefficients. For example, 3*xy* is a term, but 3 + *x* + *y* are three terms. Only **like terms** may be combined into a single term by adding. Like terms are terms that have identical variable factors. For example, 2*x* and 5*x* are like terms. So are 5*r*, 34*r*, and 15*r*. But, 2*x* and 3*y* aren't like terms.

When you add like terms, *only the numerical coefficients are added*. This idea can be shown with the following examples:

Adding like terms may be compared to adding like pieces of fruit:

2 apples + 3 apples = 5 apples

4 oranges + 6 oranges = 10 oranges

2 peaches + (a) peach = 3 peaches

(a) grape + (a) grape = 2 grapes

So:

$$2n + 3n = 5n$$

$$4x + 6x = 10x$$

$$2r + r = 3r \text{ (do you know why?)}$$

$$w + w = 2w$$

Try this one yourself:

$$2x + 3y =$$

Think of: 2 oranges + 3 grapes

You might say that 2 oranges + 3 grapes = 5 pieces of fruit, but algebra would not accept that solution. In algebraic terms:

2 oranges + 3 grapes = 2 oranges + 3 grapes

They can't be further combined. Now keeping that in mind, you should recognize that:

$$2x + 3y = 2x + 3y$$

If the variables are not the same, terms may not be combined into a single new term by adding. Only those terms containing identical variables may be added to form a single new term.

Quick Quiz D

Directions: Complete the following addition problems.

1. $4n + 3n = $ _____

2. $w + w = $ _____

3. $r + r + r = $ _____

4. $3v + 3w = $ _____

5. $\dfrac{1}{4}t + \dfrac{1}{2}t = $ _____

6. $\dfrac{z}{3} + \dfrac{z}{3} = $ _____

If you find problem 6 hard, remember that you're adding two fractions with like denominators. The common denominator is 3. Then add the 2 numerators ($z + z$) and get $2z$.

Subtracting

Subtracting variables works exactly the same as adding, except that the numerical coefficient of one variable is subtracted from the numerical coefficient of the other. All the other rules for adding variables apply.

$$4y - 2y = 2y$$

$$7m - 3m = 4m$$

$$s - s = 0$$

$$4p - 3q = 4p - 3q$$

Quick Quiz E

Directions: Solve each subtraction. Remember that z is the same as $1z$, even though you can't see the 1. Also remember that you can't combine two variables that are not like.

1. $5z - z = $ _____

2. $6x - 6x = $ _____

3. $8m - 4n = $ _____

4. $7c - 5c = $ _____

5. $9w - 4x = $ _____

6. $15v - 8v = $ _____

What Are Integers?

Before going any further, you must look at the numbers known as integers (or signed numbers). All numbers except for zero are either greater or less than zero. Those numbers that are greater than zero are called **positive numbers**, and may be written with a positive sign. For example, +6 is known as "positive six." Any number that's written without a sign in front of it is also considered to be positive. Most of the numbers you deal with in your life are positive numbers.

Numbers less than zero are called **negative numbers**. The number –6 is read "negative 6." It represents a distance six units to the left side of zero, if you're considering position on a number line:

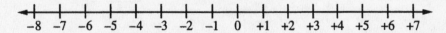

All numbers represented on a number line increase as you move from left to right and decrease as you move from right to left. So, for example, +6 is greater than +4, but –6 is less than –4. Look at the positions of these numbers on the number line above and you'll see why.

Absolute Value

The **absolute value** of a number is the distance that the number is from zero. A peek at the number line above will show you that –2 is two spaces from 0. That means that the absolute value of negative two is 2. This is how you write it out:

$$| -2 | = 2$$

The pair of vertical lines is read "the absolute value of..." Now, +2 is also two spaces away from zero, so it too has an absolute value of 2, which leads to the following conclusion:

$$| -2 | = | +2 | = 2$$

This is read: The absolute value of negative 2 equals the absolute value of positive 2 equals 2.

Quick Quiz F

Directions: Find the absolute values below.

1. $| -7 | =$

2. $| -4 | =$

3. $| +8 | =$

Where $y = -6$:

4. $| -y | =$

5. $| +y | =$

6. $| y | + 2 =$

Where $m = 7$:

7. $| m - 3 | =$

8. $| m + 2 | =$

9. $| +m + +3 | =$

How to Combine Integers

Integers can be combined by adding, subtracting, multiplying, and dividing. There are special rules that differ from non-negative numbers. For that reason, addition and subtraction will be covered separately. Multiplying and dividing follow the same rules, and so they can be looked at together.

Adding Integers

When numbers with **like signs** are added together, their absolute values are added in the usual way. The sum, however, will have the same sign that the original numbers had.

Example 1
To add:

$$+7 + (+6)$$
$$\downarrow$$
$$|+7| = 7; \quad |+6| = 6 \quad \text{Find the absolute values.}$$
$$\downarrow$$
$$7 + 6 = 13 \qquad \text{Add the absolute values.}$$
$$\downarrow$$
$$+7 + (+6) = +13 \quad \text{The sum gets the sign of the addends.}$$

(Addend is the name given to numbers being added together.)

Example 2
To add:

$$-5 + -4$$
$$\downarrow$$
$$|-5| = 5; \quad |+4| = 4 \quad \text{Find the absolute values.}$$
$$\downarrow$$
$$5 + 4 = 9 \qquad \text{Add the absolute values.}$$
$$\downarrow$$
$$-5 + -4 = -9 \quad \text{The sum gets the sign of the addends.}$$

Quick Quiz G

Directions: Add the following numbers.

1. +3 + (+7) = _____   **6.** −12 + −9 = _____

2. −4 + −8 = _____   **7.** −4 + −13 = _____

3. +5 + (+8) = _____   **8.** +12 + (+8) = _____

4. −12 + −3 = _____   **9.** −10 + −11 = _____

5. +6 + (+9) = _____   **10.** +5 + (+21) = _____

To add integers whose signs are different, you *subtract* the absolute values of the two numbers. The sum then takes the sign of the number in the addition with the greater absolute value.

You can think of the positive number as a check brought to you by your mail person, who at the same time brings you a bill. The net change in your worth would be the difference between the two. If the check were greater than the bill, you'd be better off. If the bill were greater than the check, you'd be poorer.

Example 3

$$+7 + -5$$
$$\downarrow$$
$$|+7| = 7; \quad |-5| = 5 \qquad \text{Find the absolute values} \ldots$$
$$\downarrow$$
$$7 - 5 = 2 \qquad \ldots \text{subtract them.}$$
$$\downarrow$$
$$+7 + -5 = +2 \qquad \text{The sum gets the sign of the addend with the greater absolute value.}$$

Example 4

$$+6 + -11$$
$$\downarrow$$
$$|+6| = 6; \quad |-11| = 11 \qquad \text{Find the absolute values} \ldots$$
$$\downarrow$$
$$11 - 6 = 5 \qquad \ldots \text{subtract them.}$$
$$\downarrow$$
$$+6 + -11 = -5 \qquad \text{The sum gets the sign of the addend with the greater absolute value.}$$

Quick Quiz H

Directions: Add the following numbers.

1. +3 + −4 = _____

2. −7 + (+5) = _____

3. −8 + (+9) = _____

4. −6 + −4 = _____

5. +6 + −14 = _____

6. −8 + −5 = _____

7. −9 + (+15) = _____

8. +15 + −24 = _____

9. −9 + (+9) = _____

10. −23 + (+50) = _____

Subtracting Signed Numbers

Have you ever wondered about the meaning of a double negative? Think about this sentence: I am not not going to the dentist. What does it mean to you? If you are not *not* going to the dentist, then you must be going to the dentist. The same is true of a double negative when subtracting. Two negatives actually make a positive. Here is an example:

Example 1

+12 − (−8) = ___   −(−8) is a double negative, meaning 8. So, change the example:

+12 + 8   Now you add 12 and 8 to get 20 . . .

+12 + 8 = 20   ∴ +12 − (−8) = 20

The key to subtracting signed numbers is to first deal with the subtraction sign. If a double negative is formed, replace both negatives with a single plus sign. After that, the problem is actually an integer addition problem. Study the following examples, and you'll see how each possible integer subtraction works.

Example 2

−9 − (−4) = _____   Double negative becomes a plus.

↓

−9 + 4   Then add.

↓

−9 + 4 = −5   ∴ −9 − (−4) = −5

Example 3

$$+7 - +4 = \underline{\hspace{1cm}}$$ Since taking away a gain is the same as adding a loss,
$$\downarrow$$ exchange the $-$ and $+$ signs to make $+ -$.
$$+7 + -4$$ Then add.
$$\downarrow$$
$$+7 + -4 = +3 \qquad \therefore +7 - +4 = +3$$

Example 4

$$-11 - (+3) = \underline{\hspace{1cm}}$$ For the same reason as in example 3,
$$\downarrow$$ exchange the $-$ and $+$ signs to make $+ -$.
$$-11 + (-3)$$ Then add.
$$\downarrow$$
$$-11 + -3 = -14 \qquad \therefore -11 - (+3) = -14$$

In examples 3 and 4, by exchanging the $+$ and $-$ signs, it's possible to change the subtraction problem to an addition problem. You already saw in examples 1 and 2 that a double negative changes to a plus, changing the subtraction to an addition. So, all integer subtraction problems can be turned into integer addition problems through those changes.

Quick Quiz I

Directions: Solve these subtractions by first making them into additions.

1. $-8 - (+6) = \underline{\hspace{1.5cm}}$

2. $+9 - (+4) = \underline{\hspace{1.5cm}}$

3. $+12 - (+5) = \underline{\hspace{1.5cm}}$

4. $-11 - (+20) = \underline{\hspace{1.5cm}}$

5. $+7 - (-4) = \underline{\hspace{1.5cm}}$

6. $-9 - (-6) = \underline{\hspace{1.5cm}}$

7. $+21 - (-8) = \underline{\hspace{1.5cm}}$

8. $+17 - +5 = \underline{\hspace{1.5cm}}$

9. $-16 - (-4) = \underline{\hspace{1.5cm}}$

10. $-6 - (+15) = \underline{\hspace{1.5cm}}$

Multiplying and Dividing Integers

The rules of multiplying and dividing integers are the same, so they can be treated at the same time. The signs of the integers only play a part in determining the sign of the product or quotient. To find the sign of the product or the quotient, there are exactly two rules:

1. **If the signs are the same, the sign of the answer is positive.**

2. **If the signs are different, the sign of the answer is negative.**

The following examples show how to apply these rules.

Example 1

$$+3 \times +4$$

Signs are the same,

$$\therefore +3 \times +4 = +12$$

Example 2

$$+3 \times -4$$

Signs are different,

$$\therefore +3 \times -4 = -12$$

Example 3

$$-3 \times +4$$

Signs are different,

$$\therefore -3 \times +4 = -12$$

Example 4

$$-3 \times -4$$

Signs are the same,

$$\therefore -3 \times -4 = +12$$

Here are examples for division:

Example 5

$$+15 \div +3$$

Signs are the same,

$$\therefore +15 \div +3 = +5$$

Example 6

$$+15 \div -3$$

Signs are different,

$$\therefore +15 \div -3 = -5$$

Example 7

$-15 \div +3$

Signs are different,

$\therefore -15 \div +3 = -5$

Example 8

$-15 \div -3$

Signs are the same,

$\therefore -15 \div -3 = +5$

Quick Quiz J

Directions: Solve the following, paying close attention to the signs.

1. $+5 \times +8 = $ _____

2. $-6 \times +7 = $ _____

3. $-7 \times -4 = $ _____

4. $+6 \times -7 = $ _____

5. $-12 \div +4 = $ _____

6. $-6 \div +3 = $ _____

7. $+9 \div +3 = $ _____

8. $-3 \times -8 = $ _____

9. $+30 \div -5 = $ _____

10. $+18 \div +9 = $ _____

Answers to Quick Quizzes

Answers to Quick Quiz A

All are constants except for y and $4n$.

Answers to Quick Quiz B

All are variables except for 19 and 97.

Answers to Quick Quiz C

1. 3

2. 7

3. 1

4. 19

5. 1

6. $\dfrac{2}{3}$

Answers to Quick Quiz D

1. $7n$

2. $2w$

3. $3r$

4. $3v + 3w$

5. $\dfrac{3}{4}t$

6. $\dfrac{2z}{3}$

Answers to Quick Quiz E

1. $4z$

2. 0

3. $8m - 4n$

4. $2c$

5. $9w - 4x$

6. $7v$

Answers to Quick Quiz F

1. 7

2. 4

3. 8

4. 6

5. 6

6. 8

7. 4

8. 9

9. 10

Answers to Quick Quiz G

1. +10
2. −12
3. +13
4. −15
5. +15

6. −21
7. −17
8. +20
9. −21
10. +26

Answers to Quick Quiz H

1. −1
2. 2
3. +1
4. −10
5. −8

6. −13
7. +6
8. 9
9. 0
10. +27

Answers to Quick Quiz I

1. −14
2. +5
3. +7
4. −31
5. +11

6. −3
7. +29
8. +l2
9. −12
10. −21

Answers to Quick Quiz J

1. +40
2. −42
3. +28
4. −42
5. −3

6. −2
7. +3
8. +24
9. −6
10. +2

Solving Equations 13

Staying in Balance

One of the most important concepts in algebra is that of balance. Equations need to stay balanced by doing the same math operations to both sides. It's like each side of an equation is on a scale that has to stay perfectly balanced. You have probably seen a twin pan scale like the one drawn below. Notice that the scale shown is in balance.

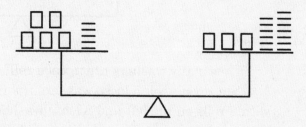

On the left arm of the scale are 5 rolls of washers and 5 loose washers. Assume that there's the same number of washers in each roll, and that the paper in which the washers are rolled has no weight. On the right arm, there are 3 rolls and 13 loose washers. Since the scale is in balance, the total weight on the left side must equal the total weight on the right.

So how many washers are there in each roll? Since the scale is balanced, you may add the same amount of weight to each side or subtract the same amount of weight from each side without changing the balance. How has the weight on the balance changed in the following picture?

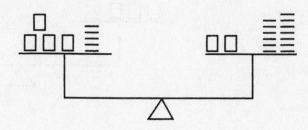

One roll has been removed from each side. The scale is still in balance. Take the maximum number of rolls possible from each side while keeping the sides in balance. Then the scale would look like this:

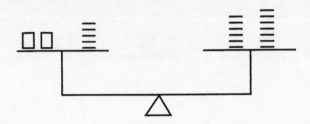

You can take two more rolls from each side. If you took another roll from the left side, you could not take another roll from the right side. There aren't any more rolls there.

Now, what is the maximum number of washers that you can remove from each side without losing the balance? Five washers can be removed.

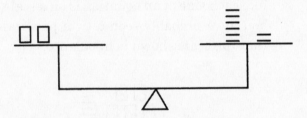

How many washers are in each roll? Can you tell now?

Since you took 5 loose washers from each side of the scale, you are left with 2 rolls on the left and 8 loose washers on the right. If 2 rolls balance 8 washers, then one roll would balance 4 washers, so there must be 4 washers in each roll.

The last balance picture was much easier to work with than the first one, since you simplified the first balance picture one step at a time.

Now look at the balance picture below. Simplify it until you can see the solution.

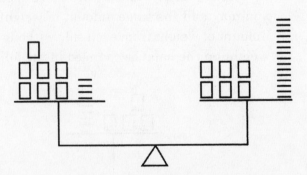

Remove 6 rolls and 4 loose washers from each side to get the simplest form for the balance picture above. It looks like this:

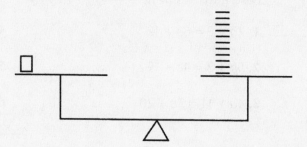

You can now see quite clearly how many washers are in a single roll.

The balance pictures are a concrete way of looking at algebra. Do you remember the first balance picture? Here it is again.

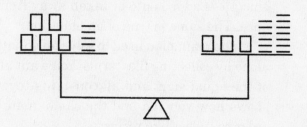

This time the rolls and loose washers will be represented by variables and constants. If you use the variable n to stand for the number of washers in each roll, you can represent the balance picture with the following sentence:

$$5n + 5 = 3n + 13$$

Try writing the math sentence for the third balance picture on the previous page. You can choose any letter to be the variable. If x is the number of washers in each roll this time, you get:

$$7x + 4 = 6x + 15$$

Math sentences are often solved in the same manner as balance pictures. Look at these two solutions:

$5n + 5 = 3n + 13$			$+7x + 4 = 6x + 15$	
$\underline{-3n \qquad -3n}$	First remove as many variables as		$\underline{-6x \qquad -6x}$	
$2n + 5 = \qquad 13$	you can from both sides of the sentence.		$x + 4 = \qquad 15$	
$\underline{\qquad -5 \qquad -5}$	Next do the same for constants.		$\underline{\qquad -4 \qquad -4}$	
$2n \quad = \qquad 8$	Now you have your solutions.		$x \quad = \qquad 11$	
$\qquad n = 4$				

Quick Quiz A

Directions: Use the solutions on the previous pages as models as you try these math sentences.

1. $7a + 8 = 6a + 12$

2. $5b + 3 = 4b + 19$

3. $4a + 11 = 3a + 20$

4. $9x + 15 = 7x + 21$

5. $8k + 9 = 6k + 25$

6. $11r + 10 = 9r + 24$

Solving Equations by Equal Additions or Subtractions

As you just saw, an algebra equation is like a scale. As long as the same amount is added onto or taken away from both sides, the scale stays in balance. The same is true of an equation.

The main plan used to solve an equation is to get the variable completely alone by collecting like terms. You want all the variables together on one side of the equal sign, and all constants together on the other side. Example 1 shows how you can add the same quantity to each side of the equation in order to collect like terms.

Example 1

$x - 5 = 14$

$\downarrow$

$$
\begin{array}{l}
x - 5 = 14 \\
\underline{+5 = +5} \\
\quad \downarrow \\
x = 19
\end{array}
$$

You don't want 5 on the same side of the equation as the x. Since 5 is combined with the x by subtracting, you add 5 (the opposite of subtracting) to *both* sides.

Example 2 shows how you can subtract the same quantity to each side of the equation in order to collect like terms.

Example 2

$n + 6 = 15$

$\downarrow$

$$
\begin{array}{l}
n + 6 = 15 \\
\underline{-6 = -6} \\
\quad \downarrow \\
n = 9
\end{array}
$$

You don't want 6 on the same side of the equation as the n. Since 6 is combined with the n by adding, you subtract 6 (the opposite of adding) from *both* sides.

In order to "move" the constant away from the variable, you'll always do the **inverse operation**. Inverse means opposite. So if the variable and the constant are *added* together, you will *subtract*. If the constant is *subtracted* from the variable, then you would *add*. The sign of the number does not affect what operation you will do, but it will affect how you add or subtract the constants. You'll use the idea of inverse operations again when you use multiplication and division in equations.

Quick Quiz B

Directions: Solve by equal additions or subtractions.

1. $r - 7 = 15$ **6.** $y - 9 = -18$

2. $x - 4 = 9$ **7.** $z + -10 = -40$

3. $m - 12 = 81$ **8.** $r - 24 = 36$

4. $x + 8 = 22$ **9.** $x - 11 = -12$

5. $k + -12 = 25$ **10.** $h + 5 = 20$

Solving Equations by Multiplication and Division

Multiplying a variable by a numerical coefficient is very common in equations. To undo a multiplication, you use the inverse (opposite) operation, which is division. Some equations show division of a variable by a constant or multiplying a variable by a fractional coefficient. They mean the same thing. In either of those cases, the simplest way to get the variable by itself is to multiply by the *reciprocal* of the coefficient. After you multiply by the reciprocal, the variable will have a coefficient of 1. Review the examples below.

Example 1

$$3a = 24$$
$$\frac{3a}{3} = \frac{24}{3}$$
$$a = 8$$

The variable, a, is multiplied by 3, so divide both sides by 3 and find that $a = \mathbf{8}$.

Example 2

$\dfrac{b}{4} = 9$ The variable, b, is divided by 4. . .

$4 \cdot \dfrac{b}{4} = 9 \cdot 4$ . . .so multiply both sides by 4. Notice the dot used as the times sign. In algebra, "x" has its own use as a variable, so the dot is used instead.

$\dfrac{4}{1} \cdot \dfrac{b}{4} = 36$ $4 = $ the fraction $\dfrac{4}{1}$ . . .

$\dfrac{4b}{4} = 36$ . . .and that makes it easier to multiply.

$\dfrac{b}{1} = 36$ The 4s divide, since $\dfrac{4}{4} = 1$ . . .

$b = 36$ . . .and so, $b = 36$.

Example 3

$\dfrac{1}{7}x = 5$ The variable x is multiplied by $\dfrac{1}{7}$. You may divide both sides

by $\dfrac{1}{7}$, but this is the same as multiplying both sides by 7,

which is $\dfrac{1}{7}$s reciprocal.

$\dfrac{7}{1} \cdot \dfrac{1}{7}x = 5 \cdot \dfrac{7}{1}$ Multiply. . .

$\dfrac{7}{1} \cdot \dfrac{1}{7}x = \dfrac{5}{1} \cdot \dfrac{7}{1}$ . . .then simplify,. . .

$\dfrac{7}{7}x = \dfrac{35}{1}$ . . .and get $x = 35$.

Example 4

$\dfrac{3}{4}x = 12$ The variable, x, is multiplied by $\dfrac{3}{4}$.

$\dfrac{4}{3} \cdot \dfrac{3}{4}x = 12 \cdot \dfrac{4}{3}$ To get a coefficient of 1, multiply by $\dfrac{4}{3}$ ($\dfrac{3}{4}$s reciprocal). . .

$\dfrac{4}{3} \cdot \dfrac{3}{4}x = \dfrac{12}{1} \cdot \dfrac{4}{3}$

$\dfrac{12}{12}x = \dfrac{48}{3}$ . . .then simplify

$x = 16$ . . .and find that $x = 16$.

Actually, whether a variable is joined to a constant by multiplying or by dividing, you can multiply by that constant's reciprocal to get the variable alone (to have a coefficient of 1). In example 1, you can consider the $3a$ (in the second step) to have been multiplied by $\frac{1}{3}$ instead of divided by 3. The two operations really do the same thing. In example 2, $\frac{b}{4}$ was multiplied by 4 because 4 is the reciprocal of $\frac{1}{4}$ and $\frac{b}{4}$ means $\frac{1}{4}b$.

Quick Quiz C

Directions: Solve the following equations by multiplying by the reciprocal of the constant. Solve for the variable.

1. $5x = 40$

2. $7n = 56$

3. $\frac{1}{2}n = 9$

4. $\frac{1}{3}r = 17$

5. $\frac{1}{8}y = 4$

6. $\frac{2}{3}m = 42$

7. $\frac{3}{4}y = 21$

8. $4v = 7$

9. $\frac{2}{3}h = \frac{3}{4}$

10. $\frac{1}{2}x = \frac{3}{4}$

Answers to Quick Quizzes

Answers to Quick Quiz A

1. $a = 4$

2. $b = 16$

3. $a = 9$

4. $x = 3$

5. $k = 8$

6. $r = 7$

Answers to Quick Quiz B

1. $r = 22$

2. $x = 13$

3. $m = 93$

4. $x = 14$

5. $k = 37$

6. $y = -9$

7. $z = -30$

8. $r = 60$

9. $x = -1$

10. $h = 15$

Answers to Quick Quiz C

1. $x = 8$

2. $n = 8$

3. $n = 18$

4. $r = 51$

5. $y = 32$

6. $m = 63$

7. $y = 28$

8. $v = 1\frac{3}{4}$

9. $h = 1\frac{1}{8}$

10. $x = 1\frac{1}{2}$

Ratios, Proportions, and Percent | 14

What Is a Ratio?

In Section II of this book, many types of fractions were listed. One of the types was as a **ratio**. A ratio is a comparison of two numbers.

There are two different ways to write ratios. One of them is with a colon, 3:4, and the other is with a fraction, $\frac{3}{4}$. Whether a colon or the fraction is used, the ratio should read "3 is to 4." Here are some common examples of ratios:

Example 1
There are 23 women and 17 men at a dance. Find the ratio of men to women, women to men, and women to people at the dance.

The ratio of men to women is 17:23 or $\frac{17}{23}$.

The ratio of women to men is 23:17 or $\frac{23}{17}$.

The ratio of women to people at the dance is 23:40 or $\frac{23}{40}$.

In any ratio, the order that the conditions are stated determines what the ratio looks like. In Example 1, three ratios were formed from just two given numbers. You can actually make six ratios from any two numbers. In all of those ratios, the order of the terms is every important. Look at Example 2 to see how the six ratios are formed.

Example 2

An order from a fast–food restaurant contains 5 hamburgers and 7 cheese-burgers. Write all of the possible ratios from this data.

Hamburgers to cheeseburgers:	5:7
Cheeseburgers to hamburgers:	7:5
Cheeseburgers to all burgers:	7:12
Hamburgers to all burgers:	5:12
All burgers to cheeseburgers:	12:7
All burgers to hamburgers:	12:5

Quick Quiz A

Directions: Form all possible ratios from the data given below.

1. 9 history teachers and 2 math teachers:

  a) history to math teachers

  b) math to history teachers

  c) math teachers to those of both subjects

  d) history teachers to those of both subjects

  e) teachers of both subjects to history teachers

  f) teachers of both subjects to math teachers

2. 19 regular letters and 2 overnight letters:

  a) regular to overnight letters

  b) overnight to regular letters

  c) regular to all letters

  d) overnight to all letters

  e) all letters to regular letters

  f) all letters to overnight letters

3. 7 orders of waffles and 3 orders of pancakes:

  a) orders of pancakes to orders of waffles

  b) orders of waffles to all orders

  c) all orders to orders of pancakes

  d) orders of waffles to orders of pancakes

  e) all orders to orders of waffles

  f) orders of pancakes to all orders

Quick Quiz B

Directions: Make 6 different ratios from each pair of numbers.

1. 4, 8 _____

2. 11, 5 _____

3. 6, 13 _____

4. 7, 12 _____

5 9, 1 _____

Quick Quiz C

Directions: Write each ratio as a fraction in lowest terms.

1. 5:9 _____   **6.** 8:4 _____

2. 6:11 _____   **7.** 9:12 _____

3. 5:17 _____   **8.** 24:36 _____

4. 7:3 _____   **9.** 18:15 _____

5. 12:4 _____   **10.** 6:9 _____

What Is a Proportion?

Ratios are useful for showing a relationship between two quantities, but they are not as useful for solving math problems. But, once two ratios are placed into a **proportion**, they become very useful. A proportion is an equation between two ratios.

6:9 = 2:3 is a proportion. It is read: "Six is to nine as two is to three." That means 6 is related to 9 *in the same way* that 2 is related to 3.

Since you don't usually see colons in math equations, but you often see fractions, proportions are almost always seen in the fraction form. The proportion above will almost always be written as $\frac{6}{9} = \frac{2}{3}$. The most important rule for proportions is that the **cross-products** are equal. Cross-products are the result of multiplying the denominator of each ratio by the numerator of the other. In this example, $9 \times 2 = 3 \times 6$, since both products are 18. This process of **cross-multiplying** will help you solve proportions where you don't know all four numerals. Here is another cross-multiplication example:

Cross-multiply: $\dfrac{1}{2} = \dfrac{4}{8}$

$$2 \times 4 = 1 \times 8$$

$$8 = 8$$

Cross-multiplication works when there is a single fraction on either side of an equal sign. That's the only time that cross-multiplication can be done.

Solving Proportions

Now that you have studied what ratios and proportions are, it's time to see how to put them to work. If you know three of the four numbers in a proportion, you can solve to find out what the fourth number is. That number will be represented by a variable.

- Step 1: Cross-multiply

- Step 2: Divide by variable's coefficient to determine the value of the variable.

Look at the example below:

$$\frac{y}{12} = \frac{4}{6}$$

$$6y = 4 \cdot 12$$

$$6y = 48$$

$$\frac{6y}{6} = \frac{48}{6}$$

$$y = 8$$

Quick Quiz D

Directions: Below are proportions, each of which has one term unknown. Find the unknown term by cross-multiplying and then solving for the variable. Solve each proportion for the variable.

1. $\dfrac{5}{8} = \dfrac{x}{40}$

2. $\dfrac{5}{12} = \dfrac{n}{60}$

3. $\dfrac{24}{15} = \dfrac{56}{n}$

4. $\dfrac{35}{40} = \dfrac{14}{r}$

5. $\dfrac{6}{7} = \dfrac{z}{8}$

6. $\dfrac{5}{9} = \dfrac{x}{12}$

7. $\dfrac{y}{9} = \dfrac{8}{11}$

8. $\dfrac{6}{k} = \dfrac{8}{13}$

9. $\dfrac{3}{v} = \dfrac{8}{21}$

10. $\dfrac{2}{9} = \dfrac{g}{8}$

Percents

Many people have difficulty understanding percents and how they work. In fact, percents are ratios, but they are easier to think of as fractions. Unlike common fractions (the kind with numerators and denominators) and decimals, percents are not based on a unit of **1.** When working with percents, one whole is represented by 100, not by the number **1.** 100% = 1 whole. Any fraction can be rewritten as a percent simply by creating a proportion:

$$\frac{\text{numerator}}{\text{denominator}} = \frac{x}{100}$$

Solving for x will then give the percent. Percents can also be called **rates**.

Example 1

Express the fraction $\dfrac{3}{4}$ as a percent.

$\dfrac{3}{4} = \dfrac{x}{100}$ First set up a proportion. . .

$4x = 300$ . . .next cross–multiply. . .

$\dfrac{4x}{4} = \dfrac{300}{4}$ . . .divide each side by 4. . .

$x = 75\%$ . . .and find the percent.

It is even easier to rewrite a decimal as a percent. Since decimals are based on the unit 1 and percents are based upon the unit 100, you just multiply the decimal by 100 and put the percent sign after it.

Multiplying by 100 is the same as moving the decimal point two places to the right.

Example 2

Express 0.35 as a percent.

$$0.35 \times 100 = z$$
$$35 = z$$
$$z = 35\%$$

Below is a table listing some equivalent fractions, decimals, and percents. It shows that any fraction can readily be expressed in any or all three forms. The decimals have been rounded to the nearest hundredth, and the percents have been rounded to the nearest whole number percent.

Fraction	Decimal	Percent
$\dfrac{10}{14}$	.71	71%
$\dfrac{2}{17}$	.12	12%
$\dfrac{1}{14}$	.07	7%
$\dfrac{4}{15}$	.27	27%
$\dfrac{3}{14}$	.21	21%
$\dfrac{4}{22}$	.18	18%
$\dfrac{6}{21}$	.29	29%
$\dfrac{2}{8}$	.25	25%
$\dfrac{9}{25}$	.36	36%
$\dfrac{8}{12}$	.67	67%
$\dfrac{8}{15}$	.53	53%
$\dfrac{9}{16}$	.56	56%
$\dfrac{4}{19}$	.21	21%
$\dfrac{8}{14}$	.57	57%
$\dfrac{2}{22}$	.09	9%

Quick Quiz E

Directions: Fill in the blanks below to write an equivalent fraction, decimal, or percent. Round all decimals to the nearest hundredth, and all percents to the nearest whole number percent.

	Fraction	Decimal	Percent
1.	_____	.83	83%
2.	$\frac{2}{10}$	_____	20%
3.	$\frac{4}{17}$	.24	_____
4.	$\frac{8}{16}$	.5	_____
5.	$\frac{4}{23}$	_____	17%
6.	_____	.45	45%
7.	_____	.67	67%
8.	$\frac{3}{10}$	.3	_____
9.	$\frac{5}{25}$	_____	_____
10.	$\frac{9}{14}$	_____	_____

Quick Quiz F

Directions: Rewrite each decimal as a percent.

1. 0.31

2. 0.12

3. 0.62

4. 0.71

5. 0.11

6. 0.6

7. 0.72

8. 0.2

9. 0.53

10. 0.06

There are two ways to write a fraction as a percent:

1. First rewrite the fraction as a decimal, and then multiply the decimal by 100 to get the percent.

$$\frac{1}{4} = 0.25$$

$$0.25 \times 100 = 25$$

$$\frac{1}{4} = 25\%$$

2. Set up the proportion with the number over the 100 missing. Solve for that missing number, and you will have the percent.

$$\frac{1}{4} = \frac{x}{100}$$

$$4x = 1 \cdot 100$$

$$\frac{4x}{4} = \frac{100}{4}$$

$$x = 25$$

$$\frac{1}{4} = 25\%$$

Quick Quiz G

Directions: Rewrite these fractions as percents. Round where needed.

1. $\dfrac{8}{21}$

2. $\dfrac{9}{18}$

3. $\dfrac{4}{6}$

4. $\dfrac{1}{6}$

5. $\dfrac{5}{8}$

6. $\dfrac{9}{17}$

7. $\dfrac{4}{12}$

8. $\dfrac{7}{15}$

9. $\dfrac{8}{9}$

10. $\dfrac{3}{10}$

Answers to Quick Quizzes

Answers to Quick Quiz A

1. a)   9:2
   b)   2:9
   c)   2:11
   d)   9:11
   e)   11:9
   f)   11:2
2. a)   19:2
   b)   2:19
   c)   19:21
   d)   2:21
   e)   21:19
   f)   21:2
3. a)   3:7
   b)   7:10
   c)   10:3
   d)   7:3
   e)   10:7
   f)   3:10

Answers to Quick Quiz B

1. 4:8, 8:4, 4:12, 8:12, 12:4, 12:8

2. 11:5, 5:11, 5:16, 11:16, 16:5, 16:11

3. 6:13, 13:6, 6:19, 13:19, 19:6, 19:13

4. 7:12, 12:7, 7:19, 12:19, 19:7, 19:12

5. 9:1, 1:9, 1:10, 9:10, 10:1, 10:9

Answers to Quick Quiz C

1. $\dfrac{5}{9}$

2. $\dfrac{6}{11}$

3. $\dfrac{5}{17}$

4. $\dfrac{7}{3}$

5. $\dfrac{3}{1}$

6. $\dfrac{2}{1}$

7. $\dfrac{3}{4}$

8. $\dfrac{2}{3}$

9. $\dfrac{6}{5}$

10. $\dfrac{2}{3}$

Answers to Quick Quiz D

1. $x = 25$

2. $n = 25$

3. $n = 35$

4. $r = 16$

5. $z = \dfrac{48}{7}$ or $6\dfrac{6}{7}$

6. $x = \dfrac{20}{3}$ or $6\dfrac{2}{3}$

7. $y = \dfrac{72}{11}$ or $6\dfrac{6}{11}$

8. $k = \dfrac{39}{4}$ or $9\dfrac{3}{4}$

9. $v = \dfrac{63}{8}$ or $7\dfrac{7}{8}$

10. $g = \dfrac{16}{9}$ or $1\dfrac{7}{9}$

Answers to Quick Quiz E

1. $\dfrac{83}{100}$

2. 0.2

3. 24%

4. 50%

5. 0.17

6. $\dfrac{9}{20}$

7. $\dfrac{67}{100}$

8. 30%

9. 0.2, 20%

10. 0.64, 64%

Answers to Quick Quiz F

1. 31%

2. 12%

3. 62%

4. 71%

5. 11%

6. 60%

7. 72%

8. 20%

9. 53%

10. 6%

Answers to Quick Quiz G

1. 38%

2. 50%

3. 67%

4. 17%

5. 63%

6. 53%

7. 33%

8. 47%

9. 89%

10. 30%

Using Percents 15

Using Percents in Real Life

Percents are commonly used in many real-life math problems. A common use of percents is finding the amount you save when an item is on sale. Another example is calculating the tip when you go out to eat. In this chapter, you'll learn how to calculate discounts, as well as the interest you earn on money in the bank.

Finding a Percent of a Number

You may remember that the multiplication words "times" and "of" mean the same thing. You have heard people say, "Your tip should be 15% of the bill." Fifteen percent of the bill is found by multiplying. But how do you multiply percents? Percents can't actually be multiplied or divided. Then how can you figure out 15 percent of the bill? The answer is in the relationship between decimals and percents. In order to find 15 percent of the bill, rewrite 15% as a decimal: 0.15. Then, you can multiply 0.15 times the amount of the bill to find the tip.

Many of the problems in this chapter will use the **percent equation** to solve them. The percent equation is a formula that you can always use to solve percent problems. To use it, you have to learn a few vocabulary terms:

- **Rate** (R) is another word for percent. The rate is always followed by the % symbol. In the percent equation, always give the rate in its decimal form, not as a percent.

- **Base** (B) is the number you are finding the *percent of*. The base is the whole amount. The word "of" almost always comes right before the base.

- **Part** (P) is the part of the whole. The part is usually right near the word "is." The percent equation looks like this: $P = R \times B$. *The part equals the rate times the base.*

Here are two examples that use the percent equation.

Example 1

Find a 15% percent tip of a $25 dinner.

(The rate is 15% and the base is $25, so you are looking for the part.)

$15\% = 0.15$	First, rewrite the percent as a decimal.
$t = 0.15 \times 25$	Then multiply the rate times the base.
$t = \$3.75$	The tip (or the part) is $3.75.

Example 2

Find 25% of 300.

(The rate is 25% and the base is 300, so you are looking for the part.)

$25\% = 0.25$	First, rewrite the percent as a decimal.
$x = 0.25 \cdot 300$	Then multiply the rate times the base. . .
$x = 75$	. . .to get the part.

Quick Quiz A

Directions: Find the missing part.

1. 30% of 944 = ___

2. 44% of 5 = ___

3. 77% of 214 = ___

4. 28% of 504 = ___

5. 38% of 925 = ___

6. 20% of 148 = ___

7. 79% of 895 = ___

8. 23% of 993 = ___

9. 57% of 553 = ___

10. 3% of 450 = ___

Percent Word Problems

There are three common types of word problems. You use the percent equation to solve these problems.

1. **"Part" Problems:** You take a percent of something in order to find a discounted price, the interest on a loan, or the tax on a sale. You are looking for the *part* in this type of problem.

2. **"Rate" Problems:** You know the cost of something both before and after a discount has been taken, and then are asked to find out what the percent discount was. You're given the part and the base, so you're looking for the *rate*.

3. **"Base" Problems:** In this problem, you know the amount of discount that was taken on an item, as well as the discounted price. You're asked to find what the original price was before the discount was taken. You're given the rate and the part, so you're looking for the *base*.

Percent word problems have many uses, most of them being in the world of business and finance. The examples below have detailed explanations, so read them carefully.

Example 1

The list price on a sport jacket is $84. It is being sold at a 23% discount. What is the sale price?

There are two ways to solve this type of problem. Both take into account that there's an original price (base), a percent discount (rate), and a reduction (lowering) of the original price by the amount of the discount (part). In other words, both multiplying and subtracting are needed. The difference in the two ways to solve the problem is the order of those two operations.

Solution 1:

First, figure the amount of the discount using the percent equation. In this case, it will be 23% of $84.

Rate = 23% = 0.23
Base = $84
Part = p
$p = 0.23 \cdot 84 = \$19.32$

Since $19.32 is the amount of the discount, you have to subtract it from the original price to find the sale price:

$84 − $19.32 = $64.68

Notice that the multiplying was done first, followed by the subtracting.

Solution 2:

This is a slightly more interesting solution since it's also useful for other types of problems. With this method, you first do the subtraction with the percent to determine what percent of the original price you will be paying. In Solution 1, you calculated the discount, but with this method you calculate the remainder that you pay for.

Since 100% is one whole, you subtract the discount percent (rate) from it to find out how much is left. If something was on sale for 20% off, you would still pay 100% − 20% (or 80%) of the price of the item. By doing this easy subtraction first, you won't have to do any subtraction at the end of the problem.

In this problem, the discount rate was 23%, so you'll first subtract that from 100%. Then use that new rate in the percent equation:

Rate = 100% − 23% = 77% = 0.77
Base = $84
Part = p
$p = 0.77 \cdot 84 = \$64.68$

Example 2

A shirt on sale costs $30. Before it was marked down, it sold for $50. Find the percent of the discount.

In this problem, you're given the part ($30) and the base ($50). Fill in the parts of the formula that you know, and then you can solve for the rate.

Rate = r

Base = 50

Part = 30

$30 = r \cdot 50$ To get r by itself, divide both sides of the equation by 50.

$\dfrac{30}{50} = r$

$0.6 = r$ Divide and you have 0.6. Rewrite 0.6 as a percent.

$60\% = r$

That means that $30 is 60% of the original price. If you are paying 60% of the original price, then the discount must have been 100% − 60%, or 40%.

Example 3

After a discount of 35%, a suit was selling for $130. What was its original selling price?

In this problem, you're given the rate (35%) and the part ($130). You're looking for the base, since you're looking for the whole original price. Since you're given the discount rate, you need to subtract it from 100%. That will give you the correct relationship between the part and the base.

Rate = 100% − 35% = 65% = 0.65

Base = b

Part = 130

$130 = 0.65 \cdot b$ To get b by itself, divide both sides by 0.65

$\dfrac{130}{0.65} = b$

$200 = b$ The original selling price was $200.

Quick Quiz B

Directions: Solve the following discount problems. Round percents to the nearest whole percent.

1. Alessandra wishes to buy a portable tape recorder that lists for $89.00. She sees it advertised as selling for 30% off. How much should she expect to pay for it?

2. Jason saw an ad for a dirt bike on sale. The ad offered a discount of 27% from the original $342 price. How much money does he need?

3. A $620 stereo was on sale at Sam Baddy's for 45% off. What was the sale price?

4. A car that listed for $8,000 was selling for $6,000. What was the percent of the discount?

5. A dining room set was on sale for $245. It had been reduced from $300. What was the percent of the price reduction?

6. A $70,000 house had been reduced for quick sale. The sale price was $53,500. What was the percent of the price reduction?

7. James bought a $575 guitar for $310. What percent did he save?

8. Melissa bought a telephone answering machine that was on sale for $204. It had been discounted by 37%. What was the answering machine's original price?

9. Francesco bought a TV set. After a 35% discount, he paid $150 for it. What was the TV's original price?

10. Kira got a 32% discount on a $43 blouse. She paid 7% sales tax. (Add this amount onto the sale price.) How much money did she have to give the cashier?

Interest Problems

Another type of percent problem deals with simple interest. Interest can be figured on money in a savings account, on stocks and bonds, on a mortgage, or on a loan. **Simple interest** assumes that interest is being paid on the amount that was originally in the account, called the **principal**. It doesn't take into account interest earned on interest.

The standard formula for figuring simple interest is: $I = p \cdot r \cdot t$

I stands for **interest** earned.

p stands for **principal** (amount of money in the account).

r is the **rate** at which the interest is paid (a percent).

t is **time** (in years).

To solve interest problems, you put what you know into the formula and solve for the variable that is missing. Any of the four variables could be missing. Since you will often work with great numbers, it is a good idea to use a calculator.

If you are asked to find the new total in an account, add the interest earned (*I*) onto the principal (*p*).

Example 1

Jakob put $5,000 into a savings certificate at 15% annual interest. What was the total amount of money in his account at the end of a year?

$I = p \cdot r \cdot t$
$p = \$5,000;\ r = 15\% = 0.15;\ t = 1$
$I = 5,000 \cdot 0.15 \cdot 1$
$I = 750$ Jakob will receive $750 interest.
$5,000 + 750 = \$5,750$ Add the interest to the principal to find the total amount in his account.

Example 2

Kendra earned $65 in interest in 2 years on her bank account that started out with $1,000 in it. What was the percent of her interest rate?

$I = p \cdot r \cdot t$
$I = \$65;\ p = \$1,000;\ t = 2$
$65 = 1,000 \cdot r \cdot 2$
$65 = 2,000 \cdot r$
$r = 0.0325 = 3.25\%$

Quick Quiz C

Directions: Solve the following interest problems.

1. Find the annual interest ($t = 1$ year) on $5,000 if the rate of interest is:

   a) 5%

   b) $12\frac{1}{2}\%$

   c) 13%

   d) $7\frac{1}{2}\%$

   e) 19%

2. Jaime earned $32 interest in one year on the $550 in his bank account. What was the annual interest rate at the bank?

3. Omar started with $1,200 in his bank account. How long would it take him to earn $100 dollars in interest if the annual interest rate is 4%?

Answers to Quick Quizzes

Answers to Quick Quiz A

1. 283.2

2. 2.2

3. 164.78

4. 141.12

5. 351.5

6. 29.6

7. 707.05

8. 228.39

9. 315.21

10. 13.5

Answers to Quick Quiz B

1. $r = 100\% - 30\% = 70\% = 0.7$
$b = \$89$
$p = 0.7 \times 89$
$p = \$62.30$

2. $r = 100\% - 27\% = 73\% = 0.73$
$b = \$342$
$p = 0.73 \times 342$
$p = \$249.66$

3. $r = 100\% - 45\% = 55\% = 0.55$
$b = \$620$
$p = 0.55 \times 620$
$p = \$341$

4. $p = \$6,000$
$b = \$8,000$
$6,000 = r \times 8,000$
$0.75 = r$
$100\% - 75\% = 25\%$ discount

5. $p = \$245$
$b = \$300$
$245 = r \times 300$
$0.82 = r$
$100\% - 82\% = 18\%$ discount

6. $p = \$53,000$
$b = \$70,000$
$53,500 = r \times 70,000$
$0.76 = r$
$100\% - 76\% = 24\%$ discount

7. $p = \$310$
$b = \$575$
$310 = r \times 575$
$0.54 = r$
$100\% - 54\% = 46\%$ discount

8. $r = 100\% - 37\% = 63\% = 0.63$
$p = \$204$
$204 = 0.63 \times b$
$b = \$323.81$

9. $r = 100\% - 35\% = 65\% = 0.65$
$p = \$150$
$150 = 0.65 \times b$
$b = \$230.77$

10. $r = 100\% - 32\% = 68\% = 0.68$
$b = \$43$
$p = 0.68 \times 43$
$p = \$29.24$

Calculate sales tax:
$r = 7\% = 0.07$
$p = 0.07 \times 29.24$
$p = \$2.05$
Add: $\$29.24 + \$2.05 = \$31.29$

Answers to Quick Quiz C

1. **a)** $I = \$5000 \cdot 0.05 \cdot 1 = \$250$

   b) $I = \$5000 \cdot 0.125 \cdot 1 = \$625$

   c) $I = \$5000 \cdot 0.13 \cdot 1 = \$650$

   d) $I = \$5000 \cdot 0.075 \cdot 1 = \$375$

   e) $I = \$5000 \cdot 0.19 \cdot 1 = \$950$

2. $32 = 550 \cdot r \cdot 1$

   $r = 0.0582 = 5.82\%$

   Jaime's interest rate was 5.82%.

3. $100 = 1200 \cdot 0.04 \cdot t$

   $100 = 48 \cdot t$

   $2.08 = t$

   It would take him 2.08 years to earn $100.

Probability, Statistics, and Graphs

Probability | 16

Probability

Probability gives you ways to deal with uncertainties. **Probability** is a numerical measure of the chance that an event will occur.

A probability value is always a number between 0 and 1. A probability of 0 means it's impossible for the event to occur. The closer a probability value is to 0, the more unlikely the event is to occur. A probability of 1 means the event will definitely occur. A probability value near 1 says that the event is almost certain to occur. Other probability values between 0 and 1 represent degrees of the likelihood that an event will occur.

In the study of probability, a **trial** is any process that gives a result. On any single trial, only one possible result will occur. Tossing a coin is a trial with two possible results: heads or tails. Rolling a die (one of two or more dice) is a trial with six possible results; playing a game of hockey is a trial with three possible results (win, lose, or tie).

Calculating Probabilities

In some trials, all possible results are equally likely. In such a trial, with n possible results, the probability of each result is $\frac{1}{n}$. For example, in the trial of tossing a fair coin, for which there are two equally likely results, the probability of each result is $\frac{1}{2}$. In the trial of tossing a fair die, for which there are six equally likely results, the probability of each result is $\frac{1}{6}$.

How would you figure the probability of getting an even number when tossing a die? There are three ways that an even number can be obtained: tossing a 2, a 4, or a 6. The probability of each one of these three results is $\frac{1}{6}$.

215

The probability of getting an even number is simply the sum of the probabilities of these three favorable results. So, the probability of tossing an even number is equal to the probability of tossing a 2, plus the probability of tossing a 4, plus the probability of tossing a 6, which is $\frac{1}{6} + \frac{1}{6} + \frac{1}{6} = \frac{3}{6} = \frac{1}{2}$.

This result leads us to the fundamental formula for computing probabilities for events with equally likely results:

The probability of an event occurring =

$$\frac{\text{The number of favorable results}}{\text{The total number of possible results}}$$

In the case of tossing a die and getting an even number, there are six possible results. Three of the results are favorable, leading to a probability of $\frac{3}{6} = \frac{1}{2}$.

Example 1

What is the probability of drawing one card from a standard deck of 52 cards and having it be a king? When you select a card from a deck, there are 52 possible results, 4 of which are favorable. Thus, the probability of drawing a king is $\frac{4}{52} = \frac{1}{13}$.

Example 2

What is the probability of drawing one card from a standard deck of 52 cards and having it be a red face-card (king, queen, jack)? When you select a card from a deck, once again, there are 52 possible results, and 6 of them are favorable (jack of hearts, queen of hearts, king of hearts, jack of diamonds, queen of diamonds, king of diamonds). Thus, the probability of drawing a red face-card is $\frac{6}{52} = \frac{3}{26}$.

Independent Events

Two events are said to be **independent** if one event happening doesn't affect the probability of the other event's happening. For example, if a coin is tossed and a die is thrown, getting heads on the coin and getting a 5 on the die are independent events. On the other hand, if a coin is tossed three times, the probability of getting heads on the first toss and the probability of getting tails on all three tosses are not independent. If heads is obtained on the first toss, the probability of getting three tails becomes 0. (The coin is tossed three times; if the first toss shows heads, only *two* tosses remain, and it is impossible to get *three* tails.)

When two events are independent, the probability that they will both happen is the *product of their individual probabilities*. For example:

The probability of getting heads when a coin is tossed is $\dfrac{1}{2}$*, and the probability of getting a 5 when a die is thrown is* $\dfrac{1}{6}$*; thus, the probability of both of these events happening is* $\dfrac{1}{2} \times \dfrac{1}{6} = \dfrac{1}{12}$*.*

In a situation where two events occur one after the other, be sure to correctly decide the number of favorable results and the total number of possible results.

Example 3

Think of a standard deck of 52 cards.

a) What is the probability of drawing two kings in a row, if the first card drawn is put back in the deck before the second card is drawn? (Hint: There are 52 cards in the deck both times.)

b) What is the probability of drawing two kings in a row if the first card drawn is not put back in the deck? (Hint: You should not get the same answer as problem 3a.)

In the first case (3a), the probability of drawing a king from the deck on the first attempt is $\dfrac{4}{52} = \dfrac{1}{13}$. If the selected card is replaced in the deck, the probability of drawing a king on the second draw is also $\dfrac{1}{13}$, and, thus, the probability of drawing two consecutive kings would be $\dfrac{1}{13} \times \dfrac{1}{13} = \dfrac{1}{169}$.

In the second problem (3b), if the first card drawn is a king and it is not replaced, there are now only three kings in a deck of 51 cards, and the probability of drawing the second king becomes $\dfrac{3}{51} = \dfrac{1}{17}$. So, the overall probability would be $\dfrac{1}{13} \times \dfrac{1}{17} = \dfrac{1}{221}$.

Quick Quiz A

Directions: Now try these problems on your own. Be sure to read them carefully.

1. A bag contains 7 blue marbles, 3 red marbles, and 2 white marbles. If 1 marble is picked at random from the bag, what is the probability that it will be red? What is the probability that it will *not* be blue?

2. A woman's change purse contains a quarter, two dimes, and two pennies. What is the probability that a coin chosen at random will be worth at least 10 cents?

3. A bag contains 4 white and 3 black marbles. One marble is selected, its color is noted, and then it is returned to the bag. Then a second marble is selected. What is the probability that both selected marbles are white?

4. Using the same set up as given in problem 3, what is the probability that both selected marbles will be white if the first marble is not returned to the bag?

5. A man applying for his driver's license estimates that his chances of passing the written test are $\frac{2}{3}$ and his chances of passing the driving test are $\frac{1}{4}$. What is the probability that he passes both tests?

6. If 2 cards are selected at random from a standard deck of 52 cards, what is the probability that they will both be diamonds?

Answers to Quick Quizzes

Answers to Quick Quiz A

1. There are 12 marbles in the bag. Since 3 of them are red, the probability of picking a red marble is $\frac{3}{12} = \frac{1}{4}$. There are 5 marbles in the bag that are not blue, so the probability of picking a marble that is not blue is $\frac{5}{12}$.

2. There are 5 coins in the purse, and 3 of them are worth at least 10 cents. Thus, the probability that a coin chosen at random will be worth at least 10 cents is $\frac{3}{5}$.

3. There are 7 x 7 = 49 ways in which 2 marbles can be selected. Since there are four ways to select a white marble on the first draw and four ways to select a white marble on the second draw, there are a total of 4 x 4 = 16 ways to select a white marble on two draws. Thus, the probability of selecting white on both draws is $\frac{16}{49}$.

4. The two selections can be made in 7 x 6 = 42 ways. Two white marbles can be selected in 4 x 3 = 12 ways. So, the desired probability is $\frac{12}{42} = \frac{2}{7}$.

5. Since these two events are independent, the probability of passing both is

$$\frac{2}{3} \times \frac{1}{4} = \frac{2}{12} = \frac{1}{6}.$$

6. The probability of drawing a diamond from the full deck is $\frac{13}{52} = \frac{1}{4}$. After the first diamond has been removed, there are 51 cards in the deck, 12 of which are diamonds. The probability of picking a diamond from this reduced deck is $\frac{12}{51}$. So, the probability of selecting two diamonds is $\frac{1}{4} \times \frac{12}{51} = \frac{1}{17}$.

Statistics 17

Statistics

Statistics is the study of collecting, organizing, and analyzing data. One of the most important statistical concepts is finding averages. In statistics, this is called **finding central tendencies**.

There are three common measures of central tendencies. The one that is the most useful (and the most common) is the arithmetic mean. It is usually just called the mean. The other two measures of central tendency are the mode and the median. All three measures are covered in this chapter.

Finding the Mean

The arithmetic **mean** is what most people call the average of a set of numbers. The problem with the word "average" is that it is not very specific. The mean, median, and mode technically are all averages. The mean is easily calculated with a calculator. First, add up all of the individual data values in a set, and then divide by the number of values in the set. Take a look at the example below.

Example 1

A researcher wants to find out the mean amount of time a certain prescription drug stays in the bloodstream of users. She examines 5 people who have taken the drug. She finds the amount of time the drug stayed in each of their bloodstreams. In hours, these times are: 24.3, 24.6, 23.8, 24.0, and 24.3. What is the mean number of hours that the drug remains in the bloodstream of these users?

To find the mean, add up all of the measured values. In this case:

$$24.3 + 24.6 + 23.8 + 24.0 + 24.3 = 121.$$

Now divide by the number of participants (5) and obtain $\frac{121}{5}$, or 24.2 hours, as the mean.

Example 2

Suppose the person with the 23.8–hour trial time had actually been measured incorrectly, and a time of 11.8 hours was the correct time. What would the mean number of hours have been?

In this case, the sum of the data values is only 109, and the mean becomes 21.8 hours:

$$24.3 + 24.6 + 11.8 + 24.0 + 24.3 = 109$$

$$109 \div 5 = 21.8$$

This example shows how much the mean can change with one incorrect piece of data. Also, one piece of data that has either a very great or a very small value can have a big impact on the mean.

Finding the Median

The **median** is another measure of central tendencies. It is not affected as much by extreme values. The median of a group of numbers is the value that's in the middle when the data values are put in numerical order. It doesn't matter whether the numbers go from least to greatest or greatest to least. This median is sometimes used instead of the mean when someone wants to reduce the impact of extreme values. The median is often used to report average home prices in a town.

Example 3

What is the median value of the data from Example 1? What is the median value of the changed data from Example 2?

In both cases, the median is 24.3. The median wasn't affected by the one small-valued observation in Example 2.

In the event that there's an even number of data values, finding the median takes an extra step. First, find the two middle values. Then, find the number halfway between those two values. In other words, find the mean of the two middle values by adding them together and dividing by 2.

Finding the Mode

The last measure of central tendency is called the mode. The mode is simply the most frequently occurring value in a series of data. In the examples above, the mode is 24.3. The mode is used when you want to know which data point (or points) occur the most often.

Quick Quiz A

Directions: Answer the following questions.

1. During the twelve months of 1998, an executive charged 4, 1, 5, 6, 3, 5, 1, 0, 5, 6, 4, and 3 business luncheons at the Wardlaw Club. What was the mean monthly number of luncheons charged by the executive?

2. Brian got grades of 92, 89, and 86 on his first three math tests. What was his mean score?

3. In order to determine the expected mileage for a particular car, the manufacturer conducts a factory test on five of these cars. The results, in miles per gallon, are 25.3, 23.6, 24.8, 23.0, and 24.3. What is the mean mileage? What is the median mileage?

4. In problem 3 above, suppose the car with the 23.6 miles per gallon actually obtained a mileage of 12.8 miles per gallon instead. What would have been the mean mileage? What would have been the median mileage?

5. An elevator is designed to carry a maximum weight of 3,000 pounds. Is it overloaded if it carries 17 passengers with a mean weight of 140 pounds?

Answers to Quick Quizzes

Answers to Quick Quiz A

1. The mean number of luncheons charged was

$$\frac{4+1+5+6+3+5+1+0+5+6+4+3}{12} = \frac{43}{12} = 3.58$$

2. Brian's mean score was $\dfrac{92+89+86}{3} = 89$ points

3. The mean mileage is $\dfrac{25.3 + 23.6 + 24.8 + 23.0 + 24.3}{5} = \dfrac{121}{5} = 24.2$ miles per

   gallon. The median mileage is 24.3 miles per gallon.

4. The mean mileage would have been $\dfrac{25.3 + 12.8 + 24.8 + 23.0 + 24.3}{5} = \dfrac{110.2}{5} =$

   22.04 miles per gallon. The median mileage would have been 24.3 miles per

   gallon, the same as it was in problem 3.

5. Since the mean is the total of the data divided by the number of pieces of data,

   that is mean $= \dfrac{\text{total}}{\text{number}}$, we have mean x number = total. So, the weight of the

   people on the elevator totals 17 x 140 = 2,380. The elevator is not overloaded.

Reading and Interpreting Graphs 18

Reading Graphs and Charts

A graph is a picture of math or statistical data. The data usually refers to a single subject or group of subjects. There are many different types of graphs:

- Pictographs
- Bar graphs
- Line graphs
- Circle graphs (or pie charts)

Every graph has a legend or key. It's usually in a small box next to the graph or along the edges of the graph. The edges of a graph are called the **axes** (pronounced ax-ees, plural of *axis*). There is a horizontal (across) axis and a vertical (up-down) axis. The key explains the meanings of the graph's information. Always find and read the key before figuring out the meaning of the graph itself. Two graphs that look identical may have very different meanings because their keys are different.

Picture Graphs

Picture graphs are also known as **histograms** or **pictographs**. Each picture on a histogram represents an amount of something. For example, a little picture of a person may stand for 500 or 1,000 people; a little car may stand for 100 automobiles, and so on. There must be a key or legend to tell you what each picture means.

Now take a look at some examples. Note that they are all based on the following graph.

Repairs Required During First Three Years for Selected TV Brands (per 100)

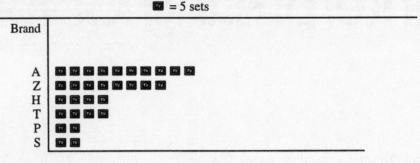

Example 1

How many more Brand A TV sets per hundred needed repair during the first three years than Brand T sets per hundred?

A careful look at the title of the graph and the key tells you what you need to know. Each TV set on the graph stands for 5 repairs per 100 sold. The row for Brand A contains 6 more symbols than the row for Brand T. Multiply 6 (symbols) × 5 (number of sets each symbol stands for) to get 30 more sets per 100.

Example 2

Which brand(s) of TV shown on the graph appear to be the most reliable?

Those brands that required the fewest repairs would be the most reliable. Two brands, P and S, have the fewest repairs. Each has 10 repairs per hundred sets.

Example 3

What percent of Brand Z televisions needed repair during the first three years?

Percent is a fraction of 100. Since the graph displays repairs per hundred sets sold, the graph actually shows percents. Each symbol represents 5%. There are 8 symbols in the Brand Z row. That means that 8 × 5%, or 40%, is the percent of Brand Z sets needing repair during their first three years.

Example 4

How many more Brand Z televisions were sold than Brand P during the three years covered by the graph?

The graph contains no information about sales records. Therefore, there is not enough information given to answer this question.

Quick Quiz A

Directions: Questions 1 to 4 refer to the following graph. (Hint: Some questions cannot be answered on the basis of the information given.)

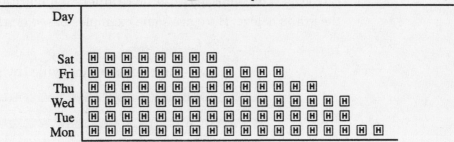

Blood Samples Taken at Beth David Hospital

Ⓗ = 10 samples

1. How many more samples were taken on Tuesday than on Thursday?

2. How many patients' blood samples revealed an illness?

3. On which two days were the same number of samples taken?

4. On which day were the samples taken half the number taken on Tuesday?

Questions 5 to 8 refer to the following graph.

Percent of Rejects per Week at ABCO Transmissions

🚗 = 1% of transmissions

Week	
6	🚗 🚗 🚗 🚗 🚗 🚗 🚗 🚗
5	🚗 🚗 🚗 🚗 🚗 🚗
4	🚗 🚗
3	🚗 🚗 🚗 🚗 🚗 🚗 🚗 🚗 🚗 🚗 🚗
2	🚗 🚗 🚗 🚗 🚗 🚗 🚗 🚗 🚗
1	🚗 🚗 🚗 🚗

5. In which week was the percentage of rejects half that of week six?

6. What is the difference in the number of transmissions rejected in week three and those rejected in week one?

7. What percentage of transmissions was rejected in week three?

8. How many more transmissions were rejected in week five than in week one?

Bar Graphs

The **bar graph** is the logical follow-up to the picture graph. It looks like a rectangle drawn around each row of pictures, with the pictures then erased. There are markings along one axis to tell you the quantity that is represented. Bar graphs can be horizontal, like most picture graphs, or vertical. Bar graphs can be used to compare two or more different quantities at the same time, as in the graph below. Here are some examples based on this graph.

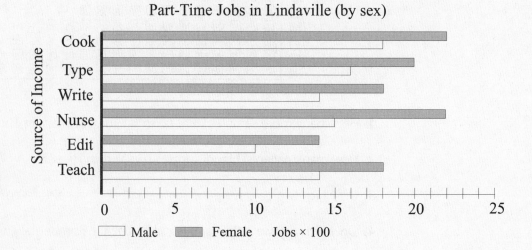

Part-Time Jobs in Lindaville (by sex)

Example 1

How many more females than males teach part-time in Lindaville?

To answer this question, first find and read the key. It tells you that the shaded bars are for females and the unshaded bars are for males. You also learn that the numbers written along the horizontal axis must be multiplied by 100. Put your finger (or better still, a straight edge) at the right end of the shaded "Teach" bar. Next, look down to the marking on the horizontal axis. It is 18. Multiplied by 100, that equals 1,800 female part-time teachers. Now do the same thing with the unshaded "Teach" bar. You should get 1,400 male teachers. Subtract to find the difference:

$$1,800 - 1,400 = 400 \text{ more female teachers.}$$

You could also subtract $18 - 14$ first, to get 4, and then multiply by 100. Your answer would still be 400 more female teachers.

Example 2

Which job has the same number of females as males whose job it is to write?

Follow the unshaded "Write" bar to its right end. Find a shaded bar that ends at the same place. You should find the shaded "Edit" bar is the same length.

Example 3

Do more females than males hold part-time jobs because more males than females in Lindaville hold full-time jobs?

The graph gives figures on part-time jobs. It says nothing about full-time jobs, and it doesn't give you reasons or explanations for the information given. There isn't enough information to answer this question.

Example 4

How many females in Lindaville work part-time as cooks or typists?

Find the right end of the shaded "Cook" bar. It ends at the 22 mark. Multiply 22 by 100, the number of jobs for which each mark stands: $22 \times 100 = 2,200$. Now repeat the same thing for the shaded "Type" bar, and you'll get 2,000. Add the two figures together: $2,200 + 2,000 = 4,200$ females who work as cooks or typists.

On the GED itself, you will not be given a ruler to help you read values off of the graphs. If you are having trouble reading a value from a graph, try using your answer sheet as a straight edge.

Quick Quiz B

Directions: Questions 1 to 4 refer to the following graph.

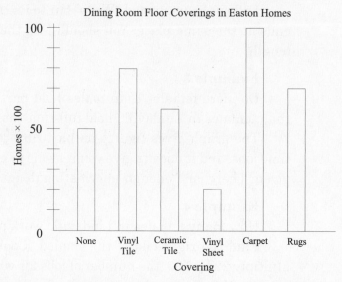

1. How many Easton homes have no floor covering in the dining room?

2. How many more Easton dining room floors have vinyl tile than ceramic tile?

3. How many Easton homes have carpeted living rooms?

4. How many Easton homes have either rugs or carpet in their dining rooms?

Questions 9 to 13 refer to the graph below.

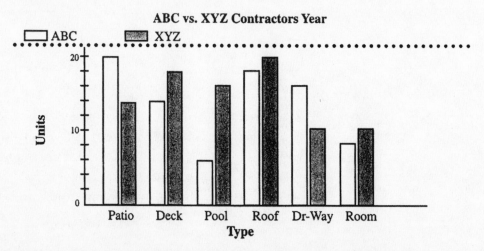

5. ABC contractors installed as many driveways last year as XYZ installed_____.

6. How many more patios did ABC contractors install last year compared to XYZ?

7. How many more roofs would you expect ABC to install this year compared to XYZ?

8. How many roofs were installed by both companies last year?

9. Which company did more jobs last year?

Line Graphs

Think of a **line graph** as being formed by drawing lines to connect the top points of vertical bars on a bar graph and then erasing the bars. Or you can think of a line graph as being created by plotting points for the values and then connecting the points. Line graphs can be used to display the same data as bar graphs. However, they're better for displaying continuous data that changes over time. For example, a line graph works well to show temperatures over a period of time or stock-price changes. It's easier to see peaks and valleys on a line graph than on a bar graph. Line graphs can also compare several sets of data.

Now take a look at the examples. They are based on the following graph.

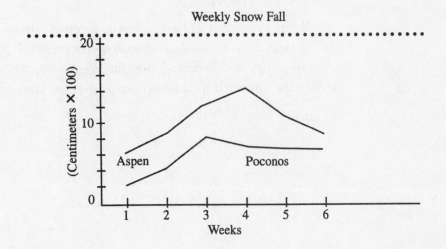

Example 1

What is the difference in the amount of snowfall in the Poconos and in Aspen in Week #3?

It helps to have two straight edges available. Move the first straight edge along the horizontal axis until it's on the Week #3 mark. Leave it there and bring the second straight edge down until it touches the "Aspen" line. Now read the snowfall on the vertical axis (each mark is 2 from the last). You should get 12. Multiply that 12 by 100 cm (from the legend):

$$12 \times 100 = 1,200 \text{ cm}$$

Now move the second straight edge down until it crosses the "Poconos" line. Read 8 on the vertical axis. Multiplied by 100 cm, that is 800 cm. To find the difference, subtract:

$$1,200 - 800 = 400 \text{ cm}$$

Example 2

For which week is the difference between the snowfall in the Poconos and in Aspen the least?

There is no need to calculate the answer to this question. The two lines are closest together at Week #6.

Example 3

For which week is the difference between the snowfall in the Poconos and in Aspen greatest?

Again, no need to measure. The lines are farthest apart at Week #4.

Example 4

For which week(s) is the snowfall in the Poconos greater than the Week #1 snowfall in Aspen?

Bring your straight edge down. Keep it square with the axes (against the vertical axis) until it reaches Aspen's snowfall for Week #1. The edge is now covering the "Poconos" line for Weeks #3, #4, and #5. Hence, in those weeks, the snowfall in the Poconos is greater than the snowfall in Aspen.

Quick Quiz C

Directions: Questions 1 to 4 refer to the following graph. (A heifer is a young cow.)

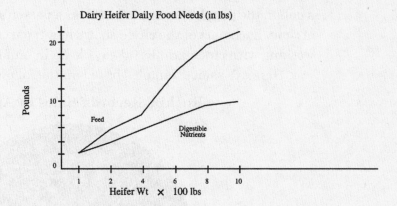

1. How many pounds of feed does a 600-lb heifer require daily?

2. What is the difference between digestible nutrients and feed needed by a 1,000-lb heifer?

3. As a heifer increases in weight, does the proportion of its food that must be digestible nutrients increase, decrease, or remain the same?

4. At what weight must all of a heifer's daily feed be digestible nutrients?

Questions 5 to 8 refer to the following graph.

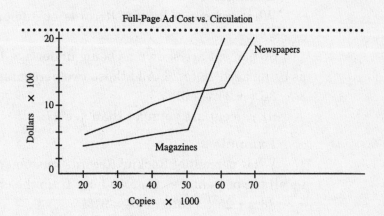

5. At what circulation does magazine advertising become more expensive than newspaper advertising?

6. What is the cost of a full-page ad in a newspaper with a circulation of 70,000?

7. What is the difference in cost between ads in magazines and newspapers with a circulation of 40,000?

8. What is the cost of an ad in a newspaper with a circulation of 10,000?

Circle Graphs

Circle graphs are also known as pie charts (one look should tell you why). They differ from other types of graphs in that they tell you about parts of a whole. Every circle chart represents a particular whole. That whole could be a dollar, the population of the world, or a person's income for a specific period of time. Each part of the circle shows how a part of that whole is used. When working with circle graphs, always keep in mind that the whole is 100%.

Here are some examples based on the following graph.

Rockin' Records' Sales by Age Group

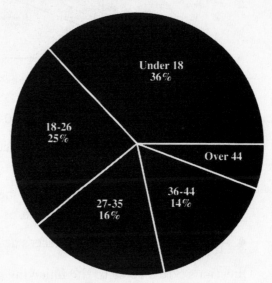

Example 1

What percent of Rockin' Records' customers are younger than 27 years of age?

36 percent are shown as being under age 18, and 25 percent are shown as being aged 18 to 26. Add those two percentages together:

36% + 25% = 61%

61 percent are younger than age 27.

Example 2

What percent of Rockin' Records' customers are over age 44? First, add up all the percentages that we have from the chart:

36% + 25% +16% +14% = 91%

The under-44 group totals 91 percent of customers. Subtract that from 100 percent to get the over-44 group:

100% − 91% = 9%

Nine percent are over age 44.

Example 3

How many of Rockin' Records' clients are aged 27 to 35?

The graph gives percentages, not numbers. With the information given, you can't answer the question.

Quick Quiz D

Directions: Now try a few circle graph questions on your own. Questions 1 to 5 refer to the following graph.

Circuit Breakers at Napa Industries

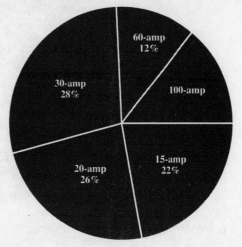

1. What is the difference in the percentages of 30-amp and 60-amp circuit breakers used at Napa Industries?

2. What percent of the breakers are 100-amp?

3. What percent of Napa breakers are less than 30-amp?

4. What percent of Napa breakers can handle 220 volts?

5. If Napa used 100 breakers, how many would be 60-amp or higher?

Questions 6 to 10 refer to the following graph.

S.O. Badd's Advertising Dollar

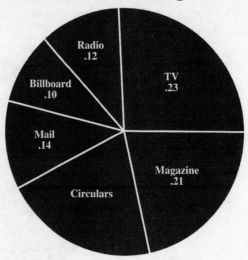

6. What percent of Badd's advertising dollar is spent on TV and radio?

7. How many cents of each advertising dollar does Badd spend on circulars?

8. If Badd spends $10,000 on advertising, how many dollars are spent on magazine ads?

9. On which advertising medium does Badd spend the most?

10. How much money does Badd spend on billboard advertising, assuming they spend $10,000 total?

Answers to Quick Quizzes

Answers to Quick Quiz A

1. 20

2. Not enough information

3. Tuesday and Wednesday

4. Saturday

5. Week one

6. Not enough information

7. 10

8. Not enough information

Answers to Quick Quiz B

1. 5,000

2. 2,000

3. Not enough information

4. 17,000

5. Pools

6. 6

7. Not enough information

8. 38

9. XYZ

Answers to Quick Quiz C

1. 16 lbs

2 12 lbs

3. Decrease

4. 100 lbs

5. 55,000+

6. $2,000

7. $400

8. Not enough information

Answers to Quick Quiz D

1. 16%
2. 12%
3. 48%
4. Not enough information
5. 24
6. 35%
7. $.20
8. $2,100
9. TV
10. $1,000

Geometry

Introduction to Geometry | 19

Geometry is the study of different types of figures, and how they relate to one another. Most of this chapter deals with **plane geometry**. A plane is a flat surface. Plane geometry deals with figures that can be drawn on a flat surface, like a piece of paper. A square, for example, is a plane figure, but a cube is not.

Some Basic Definitions

A **point** is a place in space. It takes up no space itself. Below, you see two points, *A* and *B*. The dot in each case represents, but is not actually, a point. That's because the dots occupy space, and points (as just noted) do not. A single uppercase letter is used to name a point.

A **ray** is an infinite series of points. Infinite means "going on forever without end." A ray has a single endpoint, and has direction. It's named by two points. The first point is its endpoint, and the second is another point that lies on the ray. Note from the drawings below that $\overrightarrow{CD}$ isn't the same as $\overrightarrow{DC}$. Each has a different endpoint and goes in the opposite direction.

The arrowhead on the end of each ray indicates that it continues forever in that direction.

A **line** is defined as an infinite series of points having no endpoint, as shown below. The line represented below can be called either $\overleftrightarrow{EF}$ or $\overleftrightarrow{FE}$. Unlike with rays, both names indicate the same line. Lines may **intersect** (cross) or they may never meet. Two lines in a plane that never meet are called **parallel lines**.

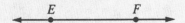

Note that *E* and *F* can be any two points on the line.

The geometric drawing that you have used the most is the **line segment**. A line segment is also an infinite series of points. However, it has two endpoints. Often, a line is incorrectly defined as the shortest distance between two points. In fact, a line segment is the shortest distance between two points. A line segment is named by its endpoints, so line segment $\overline{GH}$ is illustrated below:

$$G \bullet\!\!-\!\!-\!\!-\!\!-\!\!-\!\!-\!\!-\!\!\bullet H$$

When two rays have the same endpoint, they form an **angle**. That angle is named in two ways:

1. By using the letter of the shared endpoint of the rays

2. By naming the three points in order with the shared endpoint in the middle

The angle below can be named ∠C, ∠BCD, or ∠DCB.

The shared endpoint of the two rays is called the **vertex** of the angle. Point *C* is the vertex of angle *C*. (The plural of vertex is vertices.)

Quick Quiz A

Directions: Name each of the figures below. Also give the appropriate symbol and letter names.

1.  $\underset{E}{\bullet}\ \ \underset{W}{\bullet}\!\!\longrightarrow$

2. $\longleftarrow\!\!\underset{R}{\bullet}\ \ \underset{S}{\bullet}$

3. $\longleftarrow\!\!\underset{P}{\bullet}\ \ \underset{Q}{\bullet}\!\!\longrightarrow$

4. $\bullet M$

5. $\underset{V}{\bullet}\rule{3cm}{0.4pt}\underset{R}{\bullet}$

6.

7.

8.

9.

10.

Types of Angles and Angle Measurement

Imagine two rays, $\overrightarrow{OA}$ and $\overrightarrow{OB}$. At the start, point A is lying exactly on top of point B.

Figure 1

Pivoting at O, ray $\overrightarrow{OA}$ begins to rotate upward, forming an angle with $\overrightarrow{OB}$ at O. Before the rotation began (figure 1) the angle at O had a measure of 0°. The degree measure of an angle is based on the rotation around a point. In figure 2, the measurement of the angle is greater than 0° but less than 90°.

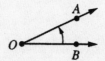

Figure 2

Figure 3 shows the ray having rotated through a quarter of a circle. The distance through which it has rotated is measured as an angle of 90°.

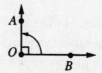

Figure 3

In figure 4, ray $\overrightarrow{OA}$ has rotated through an angle of greater than 90° but less than 180°. Figure 5 shows a rotation of 180°, or a half circle.

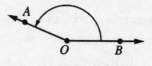   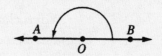

Figure 4   **Figure 5**

Angles are named based upon the amount of rotation. An angle measure less than 90° is known as an **acute angle**. An acute angle is illustrated in figure 2 (above). An angle that measures exactly 90° is a **right angle** (see figure 3, above). Figure 4 shows an **obtuse angle**, which measures greater than 90° but less than 180°. An angle measure of exactly 180° is often referred to as a **straight angle** because it looks like a line segment.

Quick Quiz B

Directions: Classify each of the following as an acute, right, obtuse, or straight angle. (It may be helpful in some cases to rotate your book in order to get a true picture.)

1.

2.

3.

4.

5.

6.

7.

8.

9.

10.

11.

12.

Triangles

Closed figures made up of line segments are known as **polygons**. The word polygon means many sides. Polygons can't have any curved sides. The simplest of the polygons is the **triangle**. A triangle is a closed figure with three sides. It is impossible to have a closed figure with fewer than three sides. Triangles may be classified in two ways:

1. By *angles*
2. By *sides*

When classified according to sides, there are three types of triangles: equilateral, isosceles, and scalene.

- An **equilateral triangle** is a triangle that has three sides of equal length.

Equilateral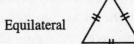

- An **isosceles triangle** has two sides of equal length.

Isosceles

Those sides are known as the legs. The non-equal side is known as the base.

- A **scalene triangle** is a triangle that has no sides equal in length.

Scalene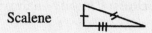

The markings on the sides of the triangles above are used to indicate equal lengths. In geometry, this is also known as **congruency**. Sides that are marked the same are **congruent** or have equal length.

When triangles are classified according to their angles, there are also three types: acute, right, and obtuse.

- An **acute triangle** has three acute angles.

Acute Triangle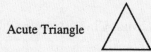

- A **right triangle** contains exactly one right angle.

Right Triangle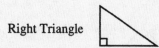

The other two angles will be acute angles. Notice the way in which the right angle is marked: this is a standard marking used to indicate that an angle is a right angle.

- An **obtuse triangle** contains exactly one obtuse angle.

Obtuse Triangle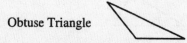

As with the right triangle, the other two angles must be acute angles.

An equilateral triangle is also equiangular. All three angles are congruent and measure 60°. Also, an isosceles triangle contains two congruent angles—those opposite the congruent sides.

The sum of the measures of all the angles of any triangle is equal to 180°. If you'd like to prove this to yourself, cut out a triangle from a piece of paper. Next, mark each of the angles in some way (a). Then, cut or tear the triangle apart, making sure not to damage any of the original angles (b). Finally, piece the three angles together with the vertices touching. You'll see that the angles total up to a straight angle (c). This will be true of any triangle, no matter whether it is acute, right, or obtuse.

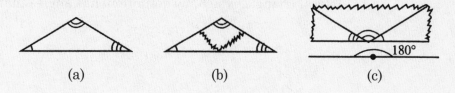

(a)   (b)   (c)

Quick Quiz C

Directions: Classify each triangle according to its sides.

1.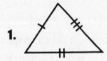

2.

3.

Directions: Classify each triangle according to its angles.

4.

6.

5.

7.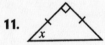

Directions: Find the number of degrees in angle *x*.

8.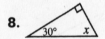
   30°   *x*

11.
    x

9.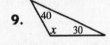
   40
   x   30

12.
    50
    x

10.
    70   *x*

13.
    x

    It might be easier to understand the answers to questions 10 through 12 by noting that those triangles are marked as isosceles. The angles opposite the congruent sides must also be congruent. Question 13 addresses an equilateral triangle, which, by definition, has angles that must be congruent.

Quadrilaterals

If you add another side to a triangle, you will get a **quadrilateral**. A quadrilateral is any four-sided polygon. Quadrilaterals, like triangles, can be classified according to certain features. One with no special features is simply known as a quadrilateral (1).

Making one pair of sides parallel in a quadrilateral makes a figure known as a **trapezoid** (2). If the other pair of legs of a trapezoid are also made parallel, a new quadrilateral is formed known as a **parallelogram** (3).

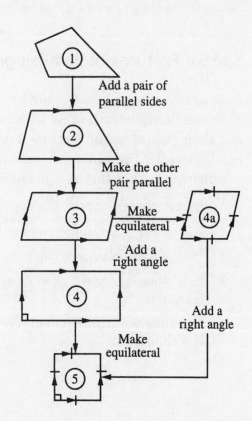

From the basic parallelogram, there are two ways to go. Right angles may be added, in which case the parallelogram becomes a **rectangle** (4). Or, make all four sides of the parallelogram congruent, and the parallelogram becomes a **rhombus** (4a).

If a rectangle is made equilateral, the result is a **square** (5). If a right angle is added to a rhombus, you also get a square. Examine the above diagram closely to see how the various quadrilaterals are related.

There are certain properties that are shared by all quadrilaterals. All have *four sides* and *four vertices* (angles). Each quadrilateral can be cut by a diagonal line segment into two triangles:

 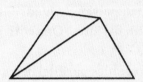 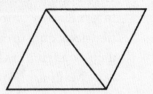

The sum of the measures of the angles in a triangle is 180°, and a quadrilateral can be cut into two triangles. So, the total number of degrees in the measures of the angles of a quadrilateral must be 360°.

Special Features of Parallelograms

Look again at the chart of quadrilaterals on the previous page. As you move down the chart, notice how each figure includes the features of the one before and then adds a special feature of its own. All the figures on the chart are quadrilaterals. The square, rhombus, and rectangle are all special kinds of parallelograms, but they're still quadrilaterals.

- In any parallelogram, the opposite sides are parallel and congruent.

- In any parallelogram, diagonally opposite angles are congruent.

- In any parallelogram, the diagonals cut each other in half.

- In a rectangle, the diagonals are congruent. (Remember, a square is a rectangle.)

- In a rhombus, the diagonals cross at right angles. (Remember a square is a rhombus.)

Quick Quiz D

The following is a group of questions based upon the features of quadrilaterals discussed above. Analyze each problem, and, if necessary, refer to the rules stated above.

Directions: State the name that most exactly identifies each type of figure.

1.

4.

2.

5.

3.

Directions: Find the value of x in each figure.

6.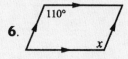

10.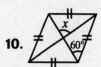

7.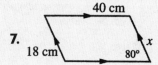

11.

8.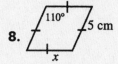

12.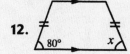

9.

Other Polygons

It's possible in theory to have a polygon of any number of sides. Here are a few other commonly used polygons:

- A five-sided polygon is a **pentagon**.

- A six-sided polygon is a **hexagon**.

- An eight-sided polygon is an **octagon**.

- A polygon of an infinite number of sides is a **circle**.

Every polygon has the same number of sides as it has vertices. So a triangle has three sides and three vertices, and a quadrilateral has four sides and four vertices. A pentagon has five sides and five vertices, etc. A **regular polygon** is defined as a polygon whose sides are all congruent and whose angles are all congruent.

Answers to Quick Quizzes

Answers to Quick Quiz A

1. ray, $\overrightarrow{EW}$

2. ray, $\overrightarrow{SR}$

3. line, $\overleftrightarrow{PQ}$ or $\overleftrightarrow{QP}$

4. point, M

5. line segment, $\overline{VR}$ or $\overline{RV}$

6. angle, ∠S, ∠TSG, or ∠GST

7. angle, ∠I, ∠HIJ, or ∠JIH

8. angle, ∠M

9. line segment, $\overline{KF}$ or $\overline{FK}$

10. line, $\overleftrightarrow{RS}$

Answers to Quick Quiz B

1. acute

2. obtuse

3. right

4. straight

5. acute

6. right

7. right

8. obtuse

9. straight

10. acute

11. obtuse

12. acute

Answers to Quick Quiz C

1. scalene

2. isosceles

3. equilateral

4. acute

5. right

6. obtuse

7. equiangular or acute

8. 60°

9. 110°

10. 70°

11. 45°

12. 65°

13. 60°

Answers to Quick Quiz D

1. rhombus

2. parallelogram

3. trapezoid

4. quadrilateral

5. rectangle

6. 110°

7. 18cm

8. 5cm

9. 120°

10. 90°

11. 85°

12. 80°

Area and Perimeter
of Basic Shapes

20

Area and Perimeter

The perimeter of a figure is the distance around the edge of that figure. A rectangle, for example, can be thought of as the fence around a rectangular-shaped space. The length of the fence is the perimeter of the rectangle.

Perimeter of Polygons

For a rectangle or a parallelogram, the perimeter is easy to compute. Rectangles and parallelograms have 2 short sides and 2 long sides. Add them together and you have the perimeter: $l + l + w + w$. However, you can take a little shortcut by multiplying and then adding:

$$P = 2l + 2w$$

The perimeter of a square or rhombus is even easier to compute, since its length and width are the same. Simply multiply the length of any side by 4:

$$P = 4s$$

For other polygons, you may have to think harder, but the process is the same. Add up the length of all the sides, and remember to label your answer with the units given in the picture.

Quick Quiz A

Directions: Find the perimeter of each figure.

1.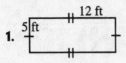

2.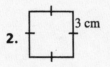

3.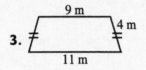

4.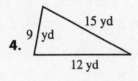

5.

6.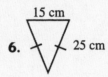

7.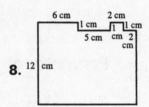

8.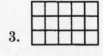

Area of Polygons

Perimeter was described as a fence around a space. Area is a way of measuring the space enclosed by the fence. The area of any region is found by dividing that region up into small squares and then counting how many squares fit into the region. For that reason, area is always expressed in **square units**, such as square inches, square feet, square meters, and so on.

Area of Rectangles and Squares

To find the area of a rectangular region that is 3 meters wide by 5 meters long, follow the steps below:

1.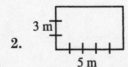

2.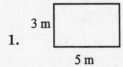

3.

Counting up the little squares, you find that the area is 15 square meters (or 15 m²). Of course, if you look back at step 1, you might see another way in which you could have found the same result. You could have multiplied the base of the rectangle by the height. (These dimensions were earlier referred to as *length* and *width*, but *base* and *height* will make it easier to talk about other shapes in a moment).

$$A = bh$$
$$A = 5 \cdot 3$$
$$A = 15 \text{ m}^2$$

Since a square is similar to a rectangle, you can use the same formula for finding its area. Multiply a square's base by its height to find its area. Since a square's base is the same length as its height, a simpler formula is possible: $A = (\text{side})^2$, but you don't need to memorize it.

Height and Perpendiculars

The term "height" was used earlier without defining it. But now you need to have a formal definition of the term. First, however, you need to understand the definition of **perpendicular**. Perpendicular lines and perpendicular line segments intersect, or cross one another, at *right (90°) angles*. Figures 1, 3, and 5 below show perpendicular lines and/or segments. Figures 2 and 4 do not.

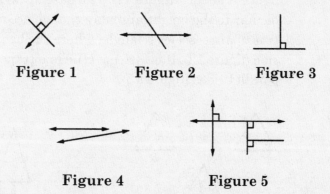

Figure 1   **Figure 2**   **Figure 3**

Figure 4   **Figure 5**

The symbol ⊥ is used to indicate that two figures are perpendicular. It's read as "is perpendicular to." Consider the case of point P and segment $\overline{AB}$ in Figure 6 below. How far is point P from $\overline{AB}$? Any of an infinite number of segments may be drawn from P to $\overline{AB}$ (figure 7). But only one of them represents the shortest distance. The shortest distance from P to $\overline{AB}$ is the perpendicular distance from P to $\overline{AB}$ (figure 8).

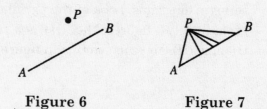

Figure 6   **Figure 7**

This segment $\overline{PQ}$ is also defined as "the distance" from the point to the line.

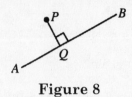

Figure 8

The **height** of a geometric figure is defined as the *perpendicular distance from the base of the figure to the opposite angle.* In the case of the rectangle, any side can be the height with respect to an adjacent side, since they're all perpendicular to one another (figure 9). In a parallelogram that isn't a rectangle, however, the height must be drawn in, as in figure 10.

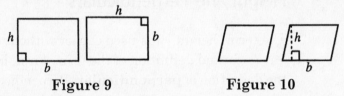

Figure 9   **Figure 10**

A triangle has three different heights, each of which refers to a different base. The base of a figure does not always refer to the side upon which the figure is sitting (figure 11). The base always refers to the side that is perpendicular to the height and may change according to convenience. (This is not true of an isosceles triangle, where the base is defined as the non-congruent side (figure 12). It is also not true in a trapezoid, where the bases are the two parallel sides (figure 13).

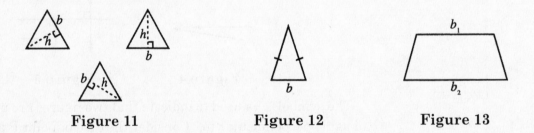

Figure 11   **Figure 12**   **Figure 13**

Area of Parallelograms

The formula for the area of a parallelogram can be developed by looking at a series of diagrams. Look at the parallelogram in figure 1. Cut that parallelogram into two figures: the first is a trapezoid (I) and the second is a right triangle (II). You can see this in figure 2.

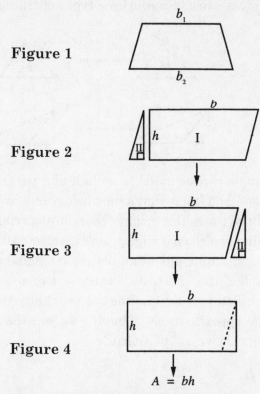

Figure 1

Figure 2

Figure 3

Figure 4

$$A = bh$$

Figure 3 shows the triangle and the trapezoid changing places. The triangle fits perfectly into the space next to the trapezoid to create a rectangle (figure 4). The new figure is identical in area to the original parallelogram.

Can you see why the base of the rectangle is identical to the base of the original parallelogram? Can you see why the height of the rectangle is identical to the height of the parallelogram? Any parallelogram can be remade into a rectangle with the identical base and height. So, the formula for the area of a parallelogram is identical to that for a rectangle:

$$A = bh.$$

Area of a Triangle

There's a special formula for finding the area of a triangle. You can figure it out from the rectangle formula. Consider any rectangle. Draw the diagonal of that rectangle, and you'll have two triangles:

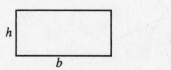 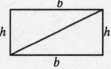

You can see that the area of either of the two triangles is half the area of the rectangle. So, the formula for finding the area of a triangle is:

$$A = \frac{1}{2}bh \ \text{or} \ A = \frac{bh}{2}$$

This formula works for all three types of triangles: scalene, acute, and right.

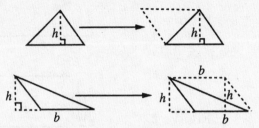

Any triangle can be made to be half of a parallelogram with the same base and height. You know that a parallelogram's area may be found by multiplying the base times the height. Therefore, a triangle's area may be computed by finding half the parallelogram's area, or half its base times its height.

Sometimes, the height of an obtuse triangle falls outside the triangle itself. Remember, the shortest distance between a point and a line is the perpendicular distance. Extend the base so that you can draw a perpendicular line to the opposite angle. That'll give you the height. The height of a triangle is also known as its **altitude**.

Quick Quiz B

Directions: Find the area of the following figures.

1.

2.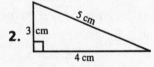

3.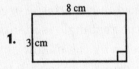

4.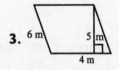

5.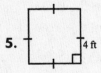

6.

7.

8.

9.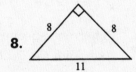

Circles

The circle is the one figure that GED geometry asks about that is not composed of line segments or rays. Circles are unique, so they have their own section.

Circumference

The longest distance across a circle is known as its **diameter**. It is labeled d in the circle below. The distance around a circle (labeled C) is known as the **circumference**. Circumference is the perimeter of a circle.

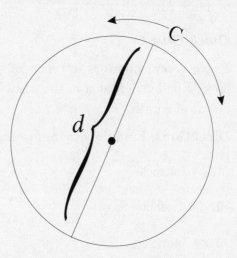

The Greeks were the ones who discovered that if they measured the length around the outside of the circle, the distance was a little more than 3 times the diameter. Today, mathematicians use computers to try to find an exact number for the ratio of a circle's circumference to its diameter. They found the ratio to equal 3.141592... and then some. This relationship has been named after the Greek letter π, known as pi (sounds like pie), and it's often estimated to the decimal 3.14 or by the fraction $\dfrac{22}{7}$. The formula for the circumference of a circle is:

$$C = \pi d$$

Any line segment that runs from the center of a circle to the edge is known as a **radius** of that circle (plural is radii). A radius is half the length of a diameter or a diameter is the length of two radii. (In case you hadn't noticed from the diagram above, the diameter passes through the center of the circle.)

Since a diameter is equal in length to two radii, there's an alternate formula for finding the circumference of a circle. The *r* stands for radius and the 2 has been moved to the front of the formula:

$$C = 2\pi r$$

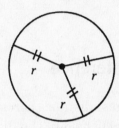

Both formulas mean the same thing, so you only need to remember one of them. After all, $2r = d$.

Quick Quiz C

Express your answers in terms of π; that means, don't substitute a number for π. Just leave it as π in the answer. Remember to label your answers with a unit of length.

Directions: Find the circumference of a circle when

1. *r* = 2 inches

2. *d* = 7 centimeters

3. *r* = 14 meters

4. *d* = 21 feet

5. *r* = 35 yards

6. *d* = 3.5 millimeters

Area of Circles

A circle's area is also found with a formula that uses the number π. The area of a circle is found by multiplying pi by the square of the radius of that circle. Squaring a number means multiplying it times itself, so $2^2 = 2 \times 2 = 4$, $3^2 = 3 \times 3 = 9$, $4^2 = 2 \times 2 = 16$, etc. The formula for finding the area of a circle is:

$$A = \pi r^2$$

Using this formula, if you know the radius of a circle to be 5, its area is 25π ($A = \pi \times 5 \times 5 = 25\pi$). Similarly, if you know the area of a circle to be 49π, then you can figure out the radius of that circle to be 7. "Unsquaring" a number is usually called "taking the square root." Think of what two identical numbers can be multiplied together to get the product that was given and you have the square root. For example, the square root of 36 is 6 since $6 \times 6 = 36$.

Quick Quiz D

Directions: For the following exercises, leave the answer in terms of π (where appropriate).

Find the area of a circle when

1. $r = 3$

2. $r = 11$

3. $d = 12$

4. $d = 14$

Directions: Find the radius of a circle when its

5. area = 64π

6. area = 100π

Coordinate Axes

On a plane surface, any point can be located by giving two coordinates, a horizontal and a vertical one. This system assumes that all flat surfaces can be covered by a grid of intersecting lines that form little squares. Each point where two lines intersect on that grid is assigned a pair of numbered coordinates. The lines from which all numbering begins are called axes (axis is the singular of axes).

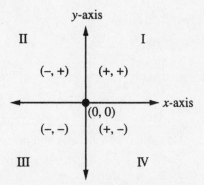

The vertical axis is known as the "**y-axis**." The y-axis meets the horizontal "**x-axis**" at the point with coordinates (0,0). Beginning at that point, known as the **origin**, all other points on the grid are assigned a pair or coordinates in the form (x,y). The coordinate written first is always the x-coordinate. It tells the horizontal distance of a point from the origin, as well as its direction from the origin. A point with a positive x-coordinate is to the right of the origin, while one with a negative x-coordinate is to the left of the origin. The y-coordinate tells the vertical distance of a point above (positive) or below (negative) the origin.

The signs written as ordered pairs on the axes above indicate which coordinate is positive and which is negative on each portion of the grid. The four sections of the grid are known as **quadrants**. In the first quadrant (I), both x and y are positive. In the second quadrant (II), x is negative and y is positive. Both x and y are negative in the third quadrant (III). The fourth quadrant (IV) is positive for x and negative for y. Here's an example:

Example 1

Consider the point with coordinates (3,5). This point is located by counting three spaces to the right of the y-axis and then 5 spaces up from the x-axis. You can see it marked on the grid below. Figure out how to plot (−2, 3) and (4,−4). What are the coordinates of point A? First, count the spaces to the left of the y-axis, and then the spaces down from the x-axis. Point A is located at (−5,−3)

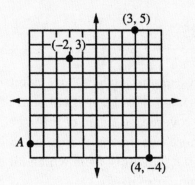

Quick Quiz E

For the exercises below, there's a grid with a number of points marked off and indicated by letters. Give the coordinates of each lettered point. It may help you to remember that the origin has coordinates (0,0).

Directions: Name each lettered point by an ordered pair of coordinates.

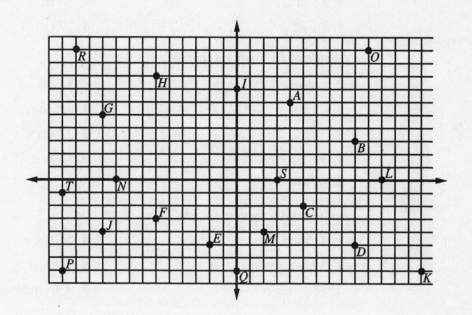

A. ___   K. ___

B. ___   L. ___

C. ___   M. ___

D. ___   N. ___

E. ___   O. ___

F. ___   P. ___

G. ___   Q. ___

H. ___   R. ___

I. ___   S. ___

J. ___   T. ___

Answers to Quick Quizzes

Answers to Quick Quiz A

1. 34 ft

2. 12 cm

3. 28 m

4. 36 yd

5. 18 dm

6. 65 cm

7. 54 m

8. 57 cm

Answers to Quick Quiz B

1. 24 cm^2

2. 6 cm^2

3. 20 m^2

4. 30 units^2

5. 16 ft^2

6. 48 m^2

7. 60 units^2

8. 32 units^2

9. 40 units^2

Answers to Quick Quiz C

1. 4π inches

2. 7π centimeters

3. 28π meters

4. 21π feet

5. 70π yards

6. 3.5π millimeters

Answers to Quick Quiz D

1. 9π

2. 121π

3. 36π

4. 49π

5. 8

6. 10

Answers to Quick Quiz E

A. (4,6)

B. (9,3)

C. (5,–2)

D. (9,–5)

E. (2,–5)

F. (–6,–3)

G. (–10,5)

H. (–6,8)

I. (0,7)

J. (–10,–4)

K. (14,–7)

L. (11,0)

M. (2,–4)

N. (–9,0)

O. (10,9)

P. (–13,–7)

Q. (0,–7)

R. (–12,10)

S. (3,0)

T. (–13,–1)

Reevaluating Your Skills

Posttest

Directions: Complete the following.

1. In the number 8,651,349,180, 5 is in the _____ place and 3 is in the
_____ place.

Solve:

2. 5,817 + 84 + 2,865 + 538 =

3. 5,754 − 4,876 =

4.
$$\begin{array}{r} 5,003 \\ -\ 4,758 \\ \hline \end{array}$$

5.
$$\begin{array}{r} 643 \\ \times\ \ 8 \\ \hline \end{array}$$

6.
$$\begin{array}{r} 87 \\ \times\ 65 \\ \hline \end{array}$$

7.
$$\begin{array}{r} 179 \\ \times\ 78 \\ \hline \end{array}$$

8.
$$\begin{array}{r} 584 \\ \times\ \ 96 \\ \hline \end{array}$$

9. $8\overline{)342}$

10. $28\overline{)8679}$

Solve the following. Express answers
in simplest form (where appropriate):

11. $\dfrac{2}{5} + \dfrac{4}{5} =$

12. $\dfrac{14}{15} - \dfrac{4}{15} =$

13. $\dfrac{7}{8} \times \dfrac{4}{21} =$

14. $\dfrac{2}{3} + \dfrac{3}{8} =$

15. $\dfrac{3}{4} - \dfrac{5}{12} =$

16. $\dfrac{4}{15} \div \dfrac{2}{5} =$

17. $\dfrac{6}{13} \div \dfrac{9}{26} =$

18. $\dfrac{15}{20} = \dfrac{\ }{4}$

19. $\dfrac{6}{7} = \dfrac{\ }{42}$

20. $3\dfrac{5}{8} = \dfrac{}{8}$

21. $6\dfrac{1}{4} + 5\dfrac{3}{8} =$

22. $7\dfrac{2}{3} - 3\dfrac{1}{4} =$

23. $4\dfrac{1}{2} \times 3\dfrac{1}{3} =$

24. $8\dfrac{3}{4} \div 5\dfrac{1}{2} =$

Express each as a decimal. If rounding is needed, round to the nearest hundredth.

25. $\dfrac{7}{100} =$

26. $\dfrac{2}{3} =$

Express as a common fraction in simplest form or as a mixed number:

27. $13.35 =$

28. $0.015 =$

Solve the following:

29. $9.5 + 1.27 + 72.6 =$

30. $61.27 - 45.88 =$

31. $0.81 \times 75 =$

32. $0.08\overline{)36.24}$

Solve for x or y:

33. $y + 11 = 39$

34. $x - 4 = -16$

Solve:

35. 30 is what percent of 80?

36. Willis bought a $7 book and paid 8% sales tax. What was his total bill?

37. Ian earned $12 interest in one year on a bank deposit at 7%. How much had he deposited?

Questions 38 to 40 refer to the graph below.

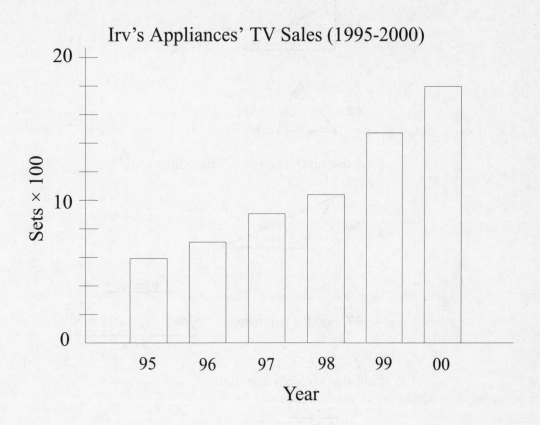

Irv's Appliances' TV Sales (1995-2000)

38. How many more TV sets were sold in 2000 than in 1995?

39. How many TV sets did Irv's sell in 1998?

40. What was the total number of TV sets sold by Irv's from 1995 through 2000?

Solve:

41. Five red jelly beans, 3 green jelly beans, and 4 yellow jelly beans are in a box. What is the probability of reaching into the box and pulling out a yellow jelly bean?

42. Using a fair coin, what is the probability of throwing 3 heads in a row?

43. Geoff, Rob, and Randy went fishing. It took Geoff 36 casts to catch a fish. Rob was much luckier, catching a fish after 18 casts. Randy got one on his 24th cast. What was the mean number of casts to catch a fish?

Name the triangles:

44.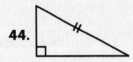

45.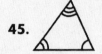

Find the total degrees of angle measure:

46.

47. Find the perimeter: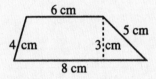

Find the area of each figure:

48.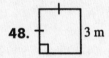

49.

50. What's the circumference of a circle with radius 9?

Answers

1. 10 millions; 100 thousands
2. 9,304
3. 878
4. 245
5. 5,144
6. 5,655
7. 13,962
8. 56,064
9. 42 R6
10. 309 R27
11. $1\frac{1}{5}$
12. $\frac{2}{3}$
13. $\frac{1}{6}$
14. $1\frac{1}{24}$
15. $\frac{1}{3}$
16. $\frac{2}{3}$
17. $1\frac{1}{3}$
18. 3
19. 36
20. 29
21. $11\frac{5}{8}$
22. $4\frac{5}{12}$

23. 15
24. $1\frac{13}{22}$
25. 0.07
26. 0.67
27. $13\frac{7}{20}$
28. $\frac{3}{200}$
29. 83.37
30. 15.39
31. 60.75
33. $y = 28$
34. $x = -12$
36. $7.56
37. $171.43
38. 1,200
39. 1,100
40. 6,600
41. $\frac{1}{3}$
42. $\frac{1}{8}$
43. 26
44. right
45. scalene-acute
46. 180°
47. 9 m²
49. 9π cm²
50. 18π

Appendix

About the GED

What to Expect on the GED

There are five GED tests:

- Language Arts, Writing
- Mathematics
- Science
- Social Studies
- Language Arts, Reading

With the exception of the Language Arts, Writing Test, all GED tests are in multiple-choice format. Each multiple-choice question will have five possible answer choices, and you must choose the best answer for each question. The multiple-choice questions may be based on a graphic, a text, or a mathematics problem, or they might just test your knowledge of a particular subject. Let's take a look at the kinds of questions asked on each subject area test:

Language Arts, Writing

The multiple-choice section of the Language Arts, Writing Test examines your knowledge of English grammar and usage. It contains several passages and accompanying questions that ask you to find errors or determine the best way to rewrite particular sentences from the passage. The essay section requires you to write a 200- to 250-word essay on a particular topic in 45 minutes. This question won't test your knowledge of a particular subject, such as the War of 1812 or the Pythagorean theorem. Instead, you are asked to write about your own life experiences. The readers of the essay will not be grading the essay based on how much you know or don't know about the topic but rather on how well you use standard English.

Social Studies

The Social Studies Test contains multiple-choice questions on history, economics, political science, and geography. In the United States, the test focuses on U.S. history and government, while the test in Canada focuses on Canadian history and government. World history is included, too. Some of the questions will be based on reading passages, and some questions will be based on graphics such as maps, charts, illustrations, or political cartoons.

Science

The Science Test contains multiple-choice questions on physical and life sciences. You will also see questions on earth science, space science, life science, health science, and environmental science. As with the Social Studies Test, some of the science questions will be based on reading passages, and others will be based on graphics such as scientific diagrams.

Language Arts, Reading

The Language Arts, Reading Test is similar to the Social Studies and Science Tests in that the multiple-choice questions will be based on passages. The passages in this test are longer than the passages in the other subject area tests. In the Language Arts, Reading Test, some of the questions will be based on poems, some on prose, some on pieces of drama, and some on documents that you might encounter in the workplace.

Mathematics

There are two parts to the Mathematics Test. You can use a calculator on Part I, but not on Part II. The Mathematics Test uses multiple-choice questions to measure your skills in arithmetic, algebra, geometry, and problem solving. Some of the questions will ask you to find the answer to a problem, while others will require you to find the best way to solve the problem. Many of the questions will be based on diagrams. Some of the questions will be grouped into sets that require you to draw upon information from a number of sources, such as graphs and charts.

The majority of GED questions on all five of the tests measure your skills and test-taking abilities. What does this mean for you? This means that if you work hard to sharpen your test-taking skills, you will be much more prepared for success on the tests than if you sat down and memorized names, dates, facts, properties, charts, or other bits of information. Basically, you will have more success on the GED if you know how to take the tests than if all you know is information about reading, writing, science, social studies, and math. Let's look at some strategies for answering multiple-choice questions.

Answering Multiple-Choice Questions

The key to success on multiple-choice tests is understanding the questions and how to find the correct answer. Each multiple-choice question on the GED will be followed by five answer choices: (1), (2), (3), (4), and (5). There will be no trick questions and no questions intended to confuse you. If you use the strategies that follow, you will be very successful on the multiple-choice questions.

Strategies for Attacking Multiple-Choice Questions

- **Read the question carefully and make sure you know what it is asking.** Read each question slowly. If you rush through the question, you might miss a key word that could cost you the correct answer. You might want to run your pencil under the question as you read it to be sure that you don't miss anything in the question. If you don't understand the question after the first time you read it, go back and read it another time or two until you understand it.

- **Don't overanalyze the question.** Many test-takers make the mistake of overanalyzing questions, looking for some trick or hidden meaning that the test-creators added for the sake of confusion. The GED creators don't do that on any of the questions, so take each question at face value. Each question will say exactly what it means, so don't try to interpret something unusual into the questions.

- **Circle or underline the key words in the question.** As you read through the question, locate any important words in the question and either circle or underline the word or words. Important words will be anything taken directly from the chart, table, graph, or reading passage on which the question is based. Other important words will be words like *compare*, *contrast*, *similar*, *different,* or *main idea*. By circling or underlining the key words, you will understand the question better and will be more prepared to recognize the correct answer.

- **After you read the question, try to answer it in your head before you look at the answer choices.** If you think you know the answer to the question without even looking at the answer choices, then you most likely will recognize the correct answer right away when you read the possible answer choices. Also, if you think you know the correct answer right away, then you should be very confident in your answer when you find it listed among the possible answer choices.

- **Try covering the answer choices while you are reading the question.** To try answering the question in your head without being influenced by the answer choices, cover the answer choices with your hand as you read the question. This technique will also help prevent you from reading something into the question that isn't there based on something you saw in one of the answer choices. Covering the answer choices may also help you concentrate only on the question to make sure you read it carefully and correctly.

- **Carefully read all the answer choices before answering the question.** You need to look at all the possibilities before you choose the best answer. Even if you think you know the answer before looking at the possible answer choices, read all of the answer choices anyway. If you read through two of the answer choices and you find that choice (3) is a good answer, keep reading because choice (4) or (5) may be a better answer. Finally, by reading all the answer choices, you can be more confident in your answer because you will see that the others are definitely incorrect.

- **Eliminate answer choices that you know are wrong.** As you read through all the choices, some will obviously be incorrect. When you find those answer choices, mark them as incorrect. This will help you narrow the possible choices. In addition, crossing out incorrect answers will prevent you from choosing an incorrect answer by mistake.

- **Don't spend too much time on one question.** If you read a question and you just can't seem to find the best or correct answer, circle the question, skip it, and come back to it later. Your time will be better spent answering questions that you can answer. Your time is limited, so don't struggle with one question if you could correctly answer three others in the same amount of time.

- **Go with your first answer.** Once you choose an answer, stick to it. A test-taker's first hunch is usually the correct one. There is a reason why your brain told you to choose a particular answer, so stand by it. Also, don't waste time debating over whether the answer you chose is correct. Go with your first answer and move on.

- **Don't go back and change your answer unless you have a good, solid reason to do so.** Remember that your first hunch is usually the best, so don't change your answer on a whim. One of the only times you should change your answer on a previous question is if you find something later in the test that contradicts what you chose. The only other time you should change an answer is if you remember very clearly a teacher's lecture, a reading passage, or some other reliable source of information to the contrary of what you chose.

- **Look for hints within the answer choices.** For example, some sets of answer choices may contain two choices that vary by only a word or two. Chances are that the correct answer is one of those two answers.

- **Watch out for absolutes.** Other hints within answer choices can be words called absolutes. These words include *always*, *never*, *only*, or *completely*. These words severely limit the possibility of that answer choice being right.

- **If you just don't know the correct answer, guess.** That's right, guess. The GED Tests are scored based on how many questions you answer correctly, and there is no point penalty for answering incorrectly. Therefore, why leave questions unanswered? If you do, you have no chance at getting any points for those. However, if you guess, you at least have a chance to get some points. Before you guess, try to eliminate as many wrong answer choices as possible. You have a much greater chance of choosing the correct answer if you can weed out some that are incorrect. This strategy is especially helpful if you have several questions left for which you are going to guess.

- **Be aware of how much time you have left on the test.** However, don't glance down at your watch or up at the clock after every question to check the time. Occasional glimpses at the clock should be sufficient to monitor your time. You will be instructed at the beginning of the test as to the amount of time you have to complete the test. Just be aware of that amount of time. The creators of the GED Tests designed the tests and test times so that you will have ample time to complete the tests. As you approach the point at which you have 10 minutes left, make sure that you are not spending your time answering the difficult questions if you still have other questions ahead of you that you can answer. If you have answered all the questions that you can with relatively little difficulty, go back and work on those that gave you trouble. If you come down to the wire and have a few left, guess at the answers. There is no penalty for wrong answers on the GED.

- **If you have time left at the end of the test, go back to any questions that you skipped.** As you just read, after you finish all the questions that you can without too much difficulty, you should go back over the test and find the ones you skipped. The amount of time you have left should determine the amount of time you spend on each unanswered question. For example, if you have 10 questions left and 10 minutes left, try to work on a few of them. However, if you have 10 questions left and 2 minutes left, go through and guess on each of the remaining questions.

What's Next?

Working with this book is the first step toward getting your GED. But what should you do next? Many people find it helpful to take a GED test-preparation course. Call your local high school counselor or the Adult Education or Continuing Education Department at your local community college, college, or university. The people in those offices can tell you where courses are offered and how to enroll. In addition to taking a GED course, continue studying on your own with this book and others in the ARCO line of books.

Once you feel ready to take the tests, contact the GED Testing Service to find out when and where the exams will be administered next:

General Educational Development
GED Testing Service
American Council on Education
One Dupont Circle, NW
Washington, DC 20036
Phone: 800-626-9433 (toll-free)
Web site: www.gedtest.org

Good luck!